THE LIBRARY OF
AMERICAN
LIVES AND TIMES™

W.E.B. DU BOIS

The Fight for Civil Rights

Ryan P. Randolph

The Rosen Publishing Group's
PowerPlus Books™
New York

To my high school history teacher, Mr. Cunningham,
for teaching his students not only the facts, but also
how to learn and ask the right questions.

Published in 2005 by The Rosen Publishing Group, Inc.
29 East 21st Street, New York, NY 10010

First Edition

Editor's Note: All quotations have been reproduced as they appeared in
the letters and diaries from which they were borrowed. No correction was
made to the inconsistent spelling that was common in that time period.

Library of Congress Cataloging-in-Publication Data

Randolph, Ryan P.
W.E.B. Du Bois: the fight for civil rights / Ryan P. Randolph.
   v. cm. — (The library of American lives and times)
Includes bibliographical references (p.) and index.
Contents: An active leader and leading intellectual —- Childhood in
Great Barrington —- To college and the reality of the South — Higher
learning and teaching — The Souls of Black Folks — Booker T.
Washington and the Niagara Conference — The NAACP and the crisis
years— Depression and action — A communist in the Cold War — Final
years in Ghana.
ISBN 1-4042-2656-7 (lib. bdg.)
1. Du Bois, W. E. B. (William Edward Burghardt), 1868–1963—Juvenile
literature. 2. African Americans—Biography—Juvenile literature. 3.
African American intellectuals—Biography—Juvenile literature. 4.
African American civil rights workers—Biography—Juvenile literature.
5. National Association for the Advancement of Colored People—
Biography—Juvenile literature. 6. African Americans—Civil rights—
United States—History—Juvenile literature. [1. Du Bois, W. E. B.
(William Edward Burghardt), 1868–1963. 2. Civil rights workers. 3.
African Americans—Biography.] I. Title. II. Series.
E185.97.D73 R36 2005
305.896'073'0092—dc22

                              2003016836

Manufactured in the United States of America

CONTENTS

1. An Active Leader and Leading Intellectual

The valuable contributions of William Edward Burghardt Du Bois to American history and literature are often forgotten outside the classroom. Du Bois was not a politician or a president as was Abraham Lincoln in the 1860s, nor was he a well-known public speaker and preacher as was Dr. Martin Luther King Jr. in the 1960s. In addition, Du Bois's later views on economics and society were often considered radical or too far from the beliefs held by mainstream America.

Born in 1868, Du Bois would live for ninety-five years until he died in 1963. His long life would span a remarkable period of history. The legacy left by the enslavement of African Americans and the American Civil War motivated Du Bois's extensive contribution to the civil rights movement and American literature. Racial violence and discrimination against black people inspired him to work toward reform. The results of

Opposite: W.E.B. Du Bois was photographed in Paris, France, in 1900. Civil rights, which Du Bois fought to obtain for African Americans, are the legal rights granted to citizens. United States citizens who are denied their civil rights can pursue a remedy in court.

Du Bois's research, writing, and activism would guide the leaders of the civil rights movement of the 1960s, when Dr. King and other social reformers would finally reverse some of the most serious civil rights injustices in America.

Du Bois was a dedicated college professor and a thoughtful writer. He wrote more than twenty books, and still more letters and articles. His scientific studies of race and culture have distinguished Du Bois as one of the founders of modern urban sociology, which is the study of people who live in city societies.

In 1903, *The Souls of Black Folk* by W.E.B. Du Bois was published. This was the first time that a book about what it meant to be an African American was published and widely read. The book is considered a classic in world literature. Du Bois was writing during a period when the still-tender wounds of the Civil War were being ripped open by racial violence and discrimination.

In addition to being a teacher and a writer, Du Bois was also a man of action. He was one of the founders of the National Association for the Advancement of Colored People (NAACP). The NAACP was instrumental in fighting for the civil rights of African Americans, and it has remained an important organization in the continuing battle for equality.

Du Bois's efforts to ensure civil rights for black people were applied not only in the United States but also in Africa. Du Bois is known as the father of Pan-Africanism.

In the early 1900s, much of Africa was divided into colonies under the control of European countries. Pan-Africanism was dedicated to promoting the unity of black Africans and their freedom from white European rulers.

Later in his long life, Du Bois supported economic and political ideas such as socialism and communism. He thought that these systems of government would bring forth a more rapid and positive change for many African Americans. These views distanced him from the civil rights movement and the African American

The NAACP and other groups staged a July 28, 1917, parade down Fifth Avenue in New York City. The marchers protested lynching and riots against African Americans, in particular a riot that had occurred a few weeks before in East St. Louis, Illinois. One banner carried in the parade read, "Mr. President, why not make America safe for democracy?"

community. During the 1950s, when Du Bois proposed these systems of government, the United States was under a threat of nuclear war from the Soviet Union, a Communist country. Many Americans, including African Americans, stood behind the U.S. government in this grave and uncertain period.

Despite these anti-Soviet feelings, Du Bois argued for peaceful relations with the Soviet Union. In 1951, Du Bois was arrested and tried for his beliefs. In his last years, Du Bois gave up his U.S. citizenship and became a citizen of the small West African nation of Ghana.

W.E.B. Du Bois was one of the greatest scholars and activists in American history. He worked, wrote, and argued tirelessly for oppressed and impoverished peoples around the world. In spite of his exile in Ghana, Du Bois remained optimistic about the potential for civil rights reform in the United States.

2. Childhood in Great Barrington

William Edward Burghardt Du Bois was born in Great Barrington, Massachusetts, on February 23, 1868. "I was born by a golden river and in the shadow of two great hills, five years after the Emancipation Proclamation, which began the freeing of American Negro slaves." This was how Du Bois recalled his childhood in his book *The Autobiography of W.E.B. Du Bois*, which was first published in the United States in 1968.

Great Barrington is a small New England town in western Massachusetts, located in the Berkshire Hills and along the Housatonic River. Nearly four thousand people lived in Great Barrington around the time that W.E.B. Du Bois was born. Most of those people were white, and it was estimated that there were fewer than thirty African American families in the area at the time.

In 1868, three years had passed since the end of the Civil War and five years had gone by since President Abraham Lincoln had freed slaves during the war. Although both sides of Du Bois's family had ancestors

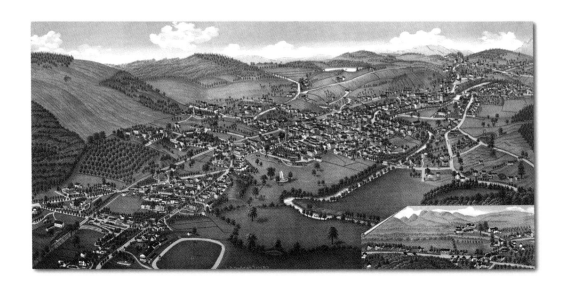

This aerial, or bird's-eye, view of Great Barrington, Massachusetts, is a lithograph that was created by L. R. Burleigh around 1884. The town is situated between two mountain ranges, the Berkshires in the east, and the Taconic in the west. Du Bois wrote of the house in Great Barrington in which he was born, "There were five rooms, a tiny porch, a rosy front yard, and unbelievably delicious strawberries in the rear."

who had been slaves, Du Bois's mother and father had been raised as free blacks.

W.E.B. Du Bois's mother was Mary Silvina Burghardt Du Bois. His mother's family was descended from Tom Burghardt. Like many slaves, Tom Burghardt had been kidnapped from his home in West Africa and had been enslaved. Dutch slave traders had taken the young boy to the Hudson River valley region of New York.

Tom was not his real name, but American or English names were usually given to slaves. Tom

Mary Silvina Burghardt Du Bois was photographed around 1868 holding her infant son William Edward Burghardt Du Bois, who went by the nickname Willie when he was a child. As he grew older, W.E.B. Du Bois would demand that people pronounce his family's last name correctly, "Due Boyss."

In this late-1500s engraving by Theodore de Bry, Dutch slave traders in Guinea, which is on the west coast of Africa, bargain for the purchase of slaves. Once these enslaved Africans were paid for, they were taken away, probably on a ship, and then sold to the Spanish.

probably took or acquired the last name Burghardt from the man who purchased him.

Tom Burghardt fought in the American Revolution. His service as a soldier for the Continental army probably won him his freedom. After the war, Tom started a family and began to farm on land that was located outside of Great Barrington, Massachusetts.

Over several generations the Burghardt family moved away from the rural life and livelihood of farming and into town, where Du Bois recalled family members taking on jobs as barbers, cooks, house-maids, waiters, and laborers.

Mary Silvina was born in 1831. She grew up in Great Barrington among the large extended Burghardt family. She left western Massachusetts only a few times in her life. Mary worked many odd jobs and often found employment as a housemaid. The hours Mary worked were long and often required strenuous labor. Du Bois considered his mother to be both patient and persevering. He remembered her as "dark shining bronze, with smooth skin and lovely eyes."

When Mary Silvina Burghardt met Alfred Du Bois, she was a bit older than the average age of marriage-able women in the 1860s. She might have thought that she had finally found her true love, or perhaps that this was her final opportunity to be married. Whatever the case, Mary was attracted to Alfred and the two were married in 1867, and a year later W.E.B. Du Bois was born.

Alfred Du Bois was not a member of a well-respected black family in Great Barrington, and, according to Du Bois, Mary's family was not pleased with the match. The Burghardts might have felt that Alfred would not provide Mary with financial security.

Alfred's father, who was Du Bois's grandfather, was named Alexander. Alexander was born in the Bahamas, the son of a white plantation owner and a black woman who was possibly a slave. As the illegitimate son of a

Alfred Du Bois posed for this photograph wearing his Union army uniform. W.E.B. Du Bois wrote in his autobiography that, after Alfred had left, his mother rarely spoke of William's father. William hesitated to ask his mother questions about Alfred. He sensed "this was a subject which hurt my mother too much even to mention."

plantation owner, Alexander was not treated as a slave. He was not, however, treated like a legitimate son by his father's family, either. Alexander did have some opportunities and was sent to school in Connecticut.

Alfred Du Bois, Alexander's son, was born in Haiti, but he later moved to New England. Alfred was light-skinned and restless. He held many jobs, such as cook, waiter, and barber in different New England towns. Alfred served in the Union army during the Civil War. Records show that by 1865 he had fled the fighting and was listed as a deserter.

Shortly after W.E.B. Du Bois's birth, Alfred left Mary and her infant child. Alfred told Mary that he was going to establish a home for the family in Connecticut. He might have actually set out to get a job and a house for the family, or, he might have been lying from the start. Mary received only one letter from Alfred. She and her son never saw Alfred again.

Without a husband, Mary worked hard to support herself and her son. "As I look back now," Du Bois recalled in his autobiography, "I can see that the little family of my mother and myself must often have been near the edge of poverty."

Du Bois attended the public school in town. Most of the children at the school were white. Du Bois was a gifted scholar and was often at the top of his class. He was also competitive and took pride in scoring better than his friends did in class. Later he described a

Du Bois's upbringing reflected the New England culture that he was exposed to as a youth. This means that his childhood training was grounded in strict rules and manners. If children disobeyed the rules, their parents often threatened them with physical punishment.

New Englanders went to church often and adhered to a strong work ethic. Emotions were not expressed outwardly because showing them was not considered proper behavior. Sometimes this way of living is called Puritan or Victorian. Although not everyone acted this way, these attitudes were common in many nineteenth-century New Englanders.

Du Bois summarized these New England values, writing, "Wealth was the result of work and saving and the rich rightly inherited the earth. The poor, on the whole, were themselves to be blamed." Although Du Bois would later change his ideas about the poor, he always believed in hard work, good manners, and showing proper respect.

W.E.B. Du Bois stands at the far left in this graduation photograph of the Great Barrington High School Class of 1884. Du Bois was the first member of the Burghardt family to graduate from high school. Du Bois's mother, Mary, emphasized the importance of education to her son.

friend from his youth named George Beebe as being, "dumb in class . . . while I was bright." He recalled a girl named Mary Dewey who "surpassed me in arithmetic," but "my grasp of history and ability to write were better than hers."

As a youth W.E.B. Du Bois took on odd jobs to earn some extra money for his mother and himself. He also spent long afternoon hours reading in Johnny Morgan's bookshop. At one point, Du Bois longed for a set of books on the history of England. Johnny Morgan allowed Du

Bois to make small payments on the books over a period of time. At Christmas, when Du Bois had made his final payment, he carried the five-volume set home.

After grade school, Du Bois went to Great Barrington High School, where he continued to excel in his studies. Sadly, despite Du Bois's academic performance, the acceptance of blacks in the white community went only so far. There was never a belief in the white community that the African American community was equal to, or even a part of, the white community. Prejudicial comments and slights against Du Bois took their toll. Du Bois would always remember a childhood incident involving a white girl, a schoolmate, who refused a visiting card from Du Bois because he was black. A visiting card was a small card that was printed with a visitor's name.

"After I entered high school, I began to feel the pressure of the 'veil of color'; in little ways at first and then in larger," he wrote. During this time W.E.B. Du Bois became interested in his race and the progress of black people in the era after the Civil War. Johnny Morgan also suggested to Du Bois that he should try writing for a local paper. Between the ages of fifteen and seventeen, from 1883 to 1885, Du Bois wrote articles for the *Springfield Republican*, an influential regional newspaper.

Du Bois also reported for the New York *Globe*, a weekly newspaper published for African Americans.

THE NEW YORK GLOBE.

Great Barrington Briefs.

GREAT BARRINGTON, Sept 23.—The political contest is near at hand, and the colored men of the town should prepare themselves accordingly. They should acquaint themselves with the political status and attitude of the candidates toward them, particularly their representatives. The choice of Governor should also demand a good share of their attention. Those who voted for Gen Butler last year "just to see what he would do," have found it a pretty costly experiment. They will see that while preaching economy and refusing the necessary appropriations to charitable institutions, he has spent an immense sum of money on needless investigations, such as Tewksbury and the like. The colored men may well ask themselves how they have been benefitted by his administration, although he professes to be their friend. A political office should not be the goal of one's ambition, but still if any one wishes an office and is worthy of it, it should not be denied him on account of his color. We had an example of this here a short time ago, when a colored man, along with a number of white men, applied for the position of night watchman. After an examination the applicants melted down to one white man, a strong Democrat, and the colored man. a Republican. A committee [composed wholly of Republicans was chosen to decide between the two candidates, and they selected the white man. The colored men of Great Barrington hold the balance of power, and have decided the election of many officers for a number of years. If they will only act in concert they may become a power not to be despised. It would be a good plan if they should meet and decide which way would be most advantageous for them to cast their votes.

...Hamilton of Pittsfield, and wife
The colored people here do not as
...lk, Conn., ...ed the proposed Colored Convention
of Albany, favorable light. **W. E. D.**
k. There ...
...cconnt of the scarcity of houses.
W. E. Du Bois.

This is a September 23, 1883, Great Barrington brief, or a short news story. It was published in the September 29, 1883, New York *Globe*. In it Du Bois advised black voters in Massachusetts to endorse candidates who would best serve their interests: "If [black voters] will only act in concert they may become a power not to be despised."

Du Bois wrote mostly about local events and the goings-on about town. In these journalistic articles, he added his own thoughts and opinions on the need for black people to organize and to become more active in politics.

In 1884, Du Bois graduated from Great Barrington High School. Du Bois wanted to continue his education and to attend Harvard University, as Harvard was considered the best university in the United States. However, Du Bois did not have the money to attend Harvard, or any other college. He might have also felt a need to stay close to his mother at home. Instead of going to college that year, Du Bois labored on a construction site.

On March 23, 1885, Du Bois's mother died at age fifty-four. Du Bois's respect for his mother's patience and dedication might have influenced his belief in women's rights, including a woman's right to vote. The loss of his mother, whom he loved and supported, was heartbreaking for young Du Bois. However, his mother's death gave him the opportunity to leave Great Barrington and explore the world.

3. To College and the Reality of the South

In 1885, a few Congregational churches in Massachusetts and Connecticut arranged a scholarship for William Edward Burghardt Du Bois. The scholarship was not awarded every year. The Great Barrington community had made a special effort for Du Bois. His academic achievements, his hard work in odd jobs, and his writing for the local newspapers had earned him respect in the small town. The church leaders decided that he should attend Fisk University in Nashville, Tennessee. Fisk University readily accepted Du Bois, thanks to his fine academic record.

Although Fisk did not have the reputation that Harvard had, it was a good college. Fisk was one of a handful of colleges that were set up after the Civil War to provide African Americans with higher education. The trip to Tennessee was Du Bois's first journey to the South. Du Bois's extended family and friends did not want him to go. He recalled, "My family and colored friends rather resented the idea. . . of sending me to the former land of slavery, either for education or for living."

The faculty and students of Fisk University in Nashville,
Tennessee, were photographed outside of Jubilee Hall around 1887.
In the enlarged detail from this group photograph, W.E.B. Du Bois
can be seen on the right.

Du Bois saw Fisk as an opportunity. "I was going
into the South; the South of slavery, rebellion, and black
folk," he wrote. After growing up with white children in
the Northeast, "I was going to meet colored people of
my own age and education, of my own ambitions."

At the age of seventeen, Du Bois entered Fisk as a
sophomore, because the education he had received at
Great Barrington High School was more advanced
than the high school education other students at Fisk
had received. Du Bois attended Fisk for three years,
between 1885 and 1888. By Du Bois's own account, he

made friends easily, despite becoming extremely ill during his first fall term at the school. He became the editor of the school paper, the *Fisk Herald*. Du Bois also deepened his love of music at Fisk, where he sang in the Mozart Society, the school's music club.

At Fisk, Du Bois saw more dramatic examples of racism, as segregation was widespread in the South. On one of his first days in Nashville, Tennessee, Du Bois recalled bumping into a white woman as he passed her on the street. When he lifted his hat to beg her pardon, the woman became upset that a black person was speaking to her as an equal.

His experience in the South led Du Bois to learn more about his race. He later recalled, "I [was] determined to know something of the Negro in the country districts; to go out and teach during the summer vacation."

Du Bois spent two summers teaching at a county school in Alexandria, Tennessee. There he witnessed firsthand the discrimination against and crushing poverty of African Americans in the South. Du Bois described his classroom as primitive: "a windowless log cabin; hastily manufactured benches, no blackboards; almost no books; long, long distances to walk."

The period that Du Bois spent teaching in the South hardened his determination to help black people who lived in extreme poverty. Despite this early exposure to poverty, later in his life, Du Bois would sometimes be criticized for having an overly intellectual and detached

(TEACHER'S COPY.)

CONTRACT WITH THE DIRECTORS OF SCHOOL DISTRICT No. _5_

State of Tennessee, County of _Wilson_ . This Contract, entered into this _11th_ day of _June_ 188_7_, between the School Directors of the _13th_ District of said County of _Wilson_ and _W. E. Du Bois_ Witnesseth: That the said Directors have engaged the said _W. E. Du Bois_ as a teacher of School No. _5_ in said District from the _13th_ day of _June_ 1887, and agree to pay _him_ the sum of _thirty_ dollars per month for _his_ services. The said _W. E. Du Bois_ agrees to give instruction in the studies required to be taught in said School and prescribed by the School Law, to such pupils as may attend the said school during the said term; to faithfully discharge the duties required by law of said school teachers, and at the close of the term, or of the period of _his_ service, to furnish the Clerk of said District with the Register of the school, said Register having been kept according to law.

R. W. Johnson Clerk } Directors.
H. C. Barry,

W. E. Du Bois Teacher.

This contract was made out to W.E. Du Bois on June 11, 1887. It specified that he was to be paid $30 per month for teaching in Wilson County, Tennessee. Du Bois wrote about his summer teaching job in the *Fisk Herald*, including an article called "How I Taught School."

attitude in his work and ideas. Some critics suggested that Du Bois was sometimes out of touch with the very people he was trying to help.

In 1888, Du Bois graduated from Fisk and wanted to continue his studies. He was intent on going to Harvard University. Luckily for Du Bois, Harvard was working to recruit students from different backgrounds and from various parts of the United States. Du Bois was accepted to Harvard as an undergraduate and began his two years of undergraduate study in the fall of 1888.

The Supreme Court is the highest judicial authority in the United States. The Court, an important part of the U.S. federal government, provides checks, or limitations, on the power of the president and of Congress.

In 1883 and 1896, the Supreme Court made two key decisions that were disastrous for African Americans and America. In 1883, the Court declared that the Civil Rights Act of 1875, which required the states to provide full and equal access for whites and blacks to all public facilities, did not apply to private institutions. This decision opened the door for "separate but equal" private facilities, such as railroads, hotels, and restaurants.

However, separate facilities for blacks were not equal to the facilities that were provided for whites. The Supreme Court failed to reverse this decision in 1896. In the 1896 case of Plessy v. Ferguson, *laws that allowed discrimination and the standard of "separate but equal" were upheld and extended to include public institutions, such as public schools.*

This 1874 lithograph, created by E. Sachse & Co., depicts Congressman Robert B. Elliott from South Carolina giving a January 6, 1874, speech before the House of Representatives. Elliot said in support of the passage of the Civil Rights Act that "Never was there a bill more completely within the constitutional powers of Congress."

Du Bois did not have many friends at Harvard and although he was probably often lonely, his isolation allowed him to concentrate on his work. Du Bois wrote, "I asked nothing of Harvard but the tutelage of teachers and the freedom of the laboratory and library. I was quite voluntarily and willingly outside its social life." Unfortunately his isolation might also have been forced upon him. Some of his classmates were unfriendly to him because of the color of his skin. Du Bois remembered that he was not allowed to join the glee club at Harvard because he was black. A glee club is a chorus of singers who gather to practice and sometimes perform short pieces of music.

At Harvard, Du Bois's most influential professor was William James, who taught both philosophy and psychology. James believed that the truth of a philosophical idea was greater if the idea could be applied to an actual situation and if the effects of the idea could be documented. Du Bois frequently spoke with Dr. James outside of class, and the professor later warned Du Bois that it would be difficult for Du Bois to make a living as a teacher of philosophy.

Du Bois graduated with honors and received his undergraduate degree in philosophy in 1890. However, he continued his studies to obtain a doctorate degree from Harvard as well. Du Bois was interested in examining relations between the black and the white races. Therefore, the focus of his doctoral research was the history of race relations. His goal was to understand the past and to change the future for African Americans.

In 1892, Du Bois decided to continue his research at

Du Bois considered the psychologist and philosopher William James, shown in a photograph, to be his "friend and [his] guide to clear thinking."

When W.E.B. Du Bois (*far right*) graduated Harvard with honors in 1890, he and five other students were chosen to give a speech at the commencement ceremony. The subject of Du Bois's speech was Jefferson Davis, the former president of the Confederate states, or those states that had withdrawn from the Union before the Civil War.

a German university. The universities in Germany had some of the best professors in all subjects, but particularly in philosophy. Although Harvard did not have a fellowship, or scholarship, to give him to study in Germany, Du Bois convinced the John F. Slater Fund for the Education of Negroes to pay for his studies abroad. The Slater Fund was a charity organized in 1882 for the education of African Americans.

"Europe modified profoundly my outlook on life and my thought and feeling toward it, even though I was there but two short years," Du Bois wrote. Du Bois felt more at ease around white people in the bigger cities of Europe. Most of the Europeans whom he met during his stay treated him like a regular person and "did not always pause to regard me as a curiosity, or something sub-human, I was a man. . . ."

This did not mean that racism did not exist in Europe, especially in the smaller towns where the population was not used to seeing black people. In one small town that Du Bois visited, a group of girls stared and giggled at him. Later as he walked through the market of this village, people followed him, pointed at him, and then talked about him as he passed by.

The University of Berlin was photographed around 1900. In 1893, Du Bois celebrated his twenty-fifth birthday in Germany. The night before his birthday, he confided his hopes and goals in a notebook and wrote that he had grand plans for "The second quarter-century of my life."

This admission card, signed by the economist Gustav Schmoller, entitled Du Bois to attend Schmoller's seminar on economics at the University of Berlin in the winter of 1893–1894. Economics is the study of how goods and services are created and then are marketed. It includes the influences that affect this process, such as the need for and availability of these goods and services.

At the end of two years, Du Bois finished his research toward his doctoral degree. He did not graduate, however, as the University of Berlin required that he take another semester of science courses. The Slater Fund would not pay for the extra classes. Therefore, in 1894, Du Bois returned to America.

4. Higher Learning and Teaching

When W.E.B. Du Bois finished his dissertation and received a doctoral degree in philosophy from Harvard in 1895, he became the first African American to receive a Ph.D. from Harvard. Du Bois had taken Harvard's required classes before he left for Germany and then officially completed his doctoral studies when the Harvard faculty approved his dissertation. A dissertation is a long piece of original research, or an original intellectual concept, which a doctoral candidate must produce to earn a Ph.D. Du Bois earned his Ph.D. in philosophy and was therefore considered to be a Doctor of Philosophy.

Du Bois's dissertation was titled "The Suppression of the African Slave-Trade to the United States of America, 1638–1870." Harvard University published his dissertation as a book in 1896. Du Bois's dissertation was a groundbreaking piece of research because he took a scientific and economic approach to a historical study of the slave trade. In his research, Du Bois went into more detail on who was involved in the slave trade and the economic numbers and forces behind it than anyone before

During his years at Harvard University, Du Bois wrote that he spent "a great deal of time in the library." This photograph of Gore Hall, which housed the Harvard library from 1841 until 1913, was taken in 1901. Until electric lamps were installed, the library was only open during the day, as the use of oil lamps was considered a fire hazard.

him had done. The book is still considered a leading source of research on the African slave trade.

While he was finishing his own research, Du Bois applied for a number of teaching positions at black colleges. He said, "I wrote no white institution—I knew there were no openings there." Finally he accepted a position as a classics professor at Wilberforce University in Ohio. Du Bois would be paid $800 per year to teach the classical languages Greek and Latin. Although Du Bois was not an expert in these languages, he knew them, as many college graduates had been taught to read and write in Greek and Latin.

While he was a teacher at Wilberforce, Du Bois met and fell in love with a student named Nina Gomer. Du Bois described her as slim, dark eyed, and beautiful. Du Bois did not write much about how he and Nina met or the initial period of their relationship. The two were married on May 12, 1896. The couple would stay together for 54 years, until Nina died in 1950.

At Wilberforce, Du Bois was able to teach and earn a living, but he was not able to conduct new research or launch programs he thought would help both the university and his career. Du Bois left Wilberforce when he was offered a special opportunity to study at the University of Pennsylvania. As an assistant instructor of sociology, Du Bois was hired to study the black population of Philadelphia's Seventh Ward. Philadelphia, Pennsylvania, was a northeastern city with a large black population and the Seventh Ward was a poor, black area of the city.

In 1896, Du Bois and Nina moved to Philadelphia and he remembered, "With my bride of three months, I settled in one room in the city over a cafeteria . . . in the worst part of the Seventh Ward. We lived there a year, in the midst of an atmosphere of dirt, drunkenness, poverty, and crime. Murder sat on our doorsteps . . . ."

Nina and Du Bois had a son in 1897 whom they named Burghardt Gomer Du Bois. Nina loved her son

Mrs. W. E. B. Du Bois.

Nina Gomer Du Bois, shown in a 1910 photograph, married W.E.B. Du Bois in May 1896. Du Bois later wrote of Nina, "Her great gift was her singularly honest character, her passion for cleanliness and order and her loyalty."

Benjamin R. Evans created this 1883 watercolor of the northwest corner of Eleventh Street and Pine Street in Philadelphia, Pennsylvania's Seventh Ward. To compile data for *The Philadelphia Negro*, Du Bois spent about eight hours per day going from door to door to interview the area's African American residents.

and spent her time tending to him and managing the household. Du Bois also adored his son and wrote, "So sturdy and masterful he grew, so filled with bubbling life."

Du Bois spent a year studying the history, economics, and culture of Philadelphia's Seventh Ward. He asked residents of the Seventh Ward about their families, education, jobs, and social activities. The research was not always easy. Du Bois wrote "The colored people of Philadelphia received me with no open arms. They had a natural dislike to being studied like a strange

Burghardt Gomer Du Bois, photographed around 1898, was the firstborn son of Nina and W.E.B. Du Bois.

species." Du Bois spent more than 800 hours conducting interviews with 2,500 families. There were almost 10,000 African Americans in the Seventh Ward at the time, and Du Bois talked with most of them.

A book with his findings, called *The Philadelphia Negro*, was published in 1899. In this book Du Bois explained that the black ghetto of Philadelphia had been created by unequal opportunities for black people. The result of such discrimination was poverty. The Philadelphia ghetto did not arise because African Americans were naturally inferior, lazy, or more likely to commit crimes. The ghetto developed because many black people did not have jobs and could not get jobs simply because they were black. Without jobs and the money that was earned from jobs, the black residents of the Seventh Ward often lived in poverty. The lack of money led to higher rates of crime. Du Bois proved his points by using scientific analysis of all the data, or factual research, that he had collected.

Many scientists and politicians who came before Du Bois began their research with the false premise, or wrong assumption, that black people were inferior to whites. Furthermore, these researchers used outdated methods and incomplete research to justify policies of segregation. For example, they would look at the high rate of crime in the Seventh Ward and conclude that blacks were more likely by nature to commit crimes. These individuals claimed that blacks possessed a criminal nature. As a result of this so-called criminal nature, they could not be treated as equals. The underlying reason for the poverty or crime in black ghettos had never been explored.

Du Bois's research was not the first in-depth study of a social group, but it was the first time that a scientific method was used in such a study. By systematically talking to almost all of the people in the Seventh Ward, by asking them similar questions, and by recording their answers, Du Bois could later look for common themes among the people in his study. Du Bois's study was certainly the first detailed examination and analysis of African Americans living in a city. Through this study, W.E.B. Du Bois became known as one of the founders of urban sociology, or the study of people and cultures in large cities.

5. *The Souls of Black Folk*

W.E.B. Du Bois's work and growing reputation helped him to get a research and teaching position at Atlanta University. He was appointed a professor of history and economics. In 1897, he moved with his wife Nina and son Burghardt to Atlanta, Georgia.

After the family had been living in Atlanta for about a year and a half, Burghardt died of diphtheria at age two. The child might have gotten sick from Atlanta's water, which was often polluted by the city's sewage system. Burghardt suffered ten days of high fever. At the time, Du Bois was preoccupied with his new job and thought that Burghardt had a passing illness and would soon recover. The night before the child died, Du Bois tried in vain to find one of the few black doctors in Atlanta. No white doctors would tend to a sick black baby.

Nina, Burghardt's mother, never really recovered from the loss of her son. She blamed Du Bois for not paying enough attention when Burghardt became ill. The emotional trauma of the event had an impact on Nina and Du Bois for a long time.

Rev. Horace Bumstead, D. D.,
PRESIDENT.

Rev. M. W. Adams, Ph. D.,
DEAN.

ATLANTA UNIVERSITY.

Atlanta, Ga., 5 — Jan. 1902

Dear Will:

I don't suppose you've been up very long as this is sunday morning. It's a bit cold here, Mrs. Brice says its very cold.

Every thing seems to be going on all right from what I can hear. Mrs Francis, Miss Clifford and Miss Greene have called since you left.

I didn't know wheather you wanted to see these papers from the students or not so have sent you some and send two to-day with my letter.

Yolande comes in your room and looks about but she seems to know you're gone for when I ask her where you are she looks as indignant as though she thought why I know he's gone away and its useless to look for him.

Your
Nina

Nina Du Bois wrote this January 5, 1902, letter to her husband. Nina tells Du Bois that their two-year old daughter Nina Yolande "comes in your room and looks about but she seems to know you're gone for when I ask her where you are she looks [annoyed] as though she [knows her father has] gone away and it's useless to look for him."

Nina and Du Bois had another child. Their daughter, Nina Yolande, was born on October 21, 1900. Yolande's arrival would bring the couple closer together. However, Du Bois remained busy with his research and his teaching at Atlanta University. He spent increasingly less time with his family. Nina tried to connect with Du Bois by writing him occasional notes and letters about small happenings around the house or observations about their daughter.

Yolande would later make her own attempts to grab her father's attention, by doing such things as misbehaving at school. Yet Nina was usually the more concerned parent, not Du Bois. Du Bois loved his daughter and had high expectations for her to become an educated, independent woman. Nevertheless, his high hopes for her future did not mean that he gave her the fatherly attention she needed as a child.

Du Bois spent a great deal of time focusing on the problems that African Americans faced, including racial violence. Between 1882 and 1930, about 3,300 African Americans were lynched, mostly in the South. There were more than 161 lynchings of black people in 1892, the year Du Bois returned from Europe. Lynching is the murder of an individual by a mob, usually by hanging. These acts were designed to terrorize African Americans. Though these terrorist activities were illegal, the laws that prohibited mob violence were never enforced. Often many of the white men in the mob were also political leaders.

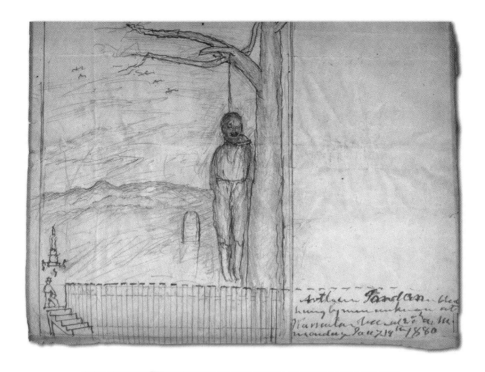

Dr. Gustavus Richard Brown Horner was an author who kept a diary. Horner made this sketch after Arthur Jordan was lynched by fifty masked men in a Virginian cemetery the previous night. The caption on the lower right of this sketch reads: "Arthur Jordan . . . hung by men unknown at Warrenton . . . 2 o'clock a.m. Monday Jan. 19th 1880."

In April 1899, a black farmer named Sam Hose fatally shot a white man in an argument over money. When Du Bois heard that Hose had been arrested, he wrote a letter appealing to the citizens of Atlanta that lynching was wrong and unjust. Du Bois hoped this letter would be published in the Atlanta newspaper *Constitution*. Before Du Bois could deliver the letter, Sam Hose was lynched and his body was burned by a mob of about two thousand people. Du Bois recalled in his autobiography, "One could not be a calm, cool, and detached scientist while Negroes

Between 1877 and 1965, most southern states passed and maintained Jim Crow laws to discriminate against blacks. Jim Crow refers to a stereotypical African American character common in the traveling minstrel plays of the late 1800s.

A Jim Crow law is any law that legalized the segregation of races in some activity, such as schooling, transportation, or marriage. Many of these discriminatory laws were passed between 1895 and 1909.

were murdered, lynched, and starved."

Du Bois would express his frustration, sadness, and personal experience from this period in a collection of fourteen essays called *The Souls of Black Folk*. By relating his own experience on paper, Du Bois also captured the emotions of millions of other African Americans who had encountered similar discrimination and threats because of their race. This book gave voice to the joys, disappointments, and sorrows of African Americans.

The Souls of Black Folk was published in 1903 by A. C. McClurg and Company in Chicago, Illinois, and became an immediate success. Nine of the fourteen essays had been published previously in magazines such as the

The 1903 first edition of *The Souls of Black Folk* included an engraving of Du Bois's signature. The book contains an essay called "Of the Passing of the First-Born," in which Du Bois expresses his grief over the loss of his son: "He died at eventide, when the sun lay like a brooding sorrow above the western hills, veiling its face; when the winds spoke not, and the trees, the great green trees he loved, stood motionless."

Atlantic Monthly and *Dial*. The book received positive reviews from many people, particularly in African American newspapers.

In the book's first essay, "Of Our Spiritual Strivings," Du Bois reflected on the dual consciousness felt by African Americans. "One ever feels his two-ness, — an American, a Negro; two souls, two thoughts . . . two warring ideals in one dark body. . . ." This idea captured the feelings of many African Americans, who were Americans, but who were also part of their own culture. Being an African American in an American society that allowed segregation, that did not punish lynchings, and that did not permit African Americans to vote was an everyday struggle.

In addition to writing and continuing his research at Atlanta University, W.E.B. Du Bois began to explore the problem of race relations globally. In Du Bois's time, several European countries and the United States had colonies. Colonialism means that the government of one country controls the people of another country. Sometimes colonies are called territories or protectorates. In 1900, most of Africa was divided into colonies in which European countries controlled the largely black populations.

Opposite page: This map of Africa by Sir Edward Hertslet was published in London, England, in 1909. The map depicts the colonization of Africa by other nations. The African land that was claimed by these nations can be identified in the color-coded map key at the lower left.

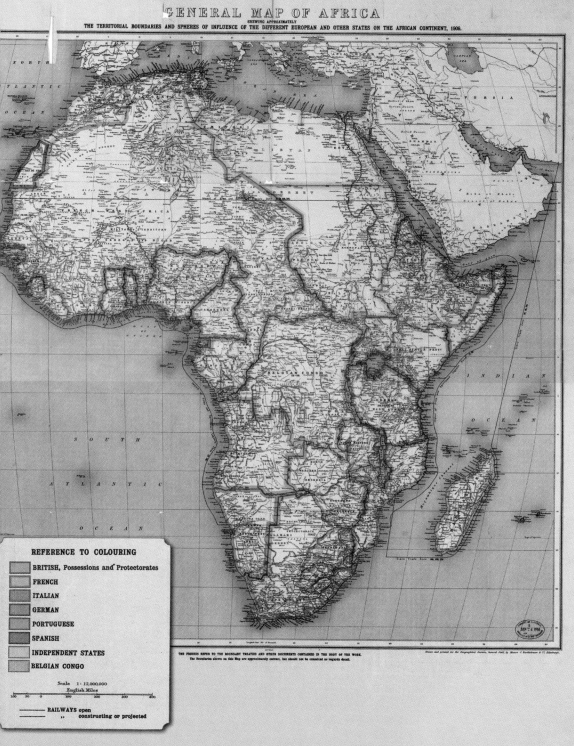

GENERAL MAP OF AFRICA
SHEWING APPROXIMATELY
THE TERRITORIAL BOUNDARIES AND SPHERES OF INFLUENCE OF THE DIFFERENT EUROPEAN AND OTHER STATES ON THE AFRICAN CONTINENT, 1909.

REFERENCE TO COLOURING

- BRITISH, Possessions and Protectorates
- FRENCH
- ITALIAN
- GERMAN
- PORTUGUESE
- SPANISH
- INDEPENDENT STATES
- BELGIAN CONGO

Scale 1 : 12,000,000
English Miles

RAILWAYS open
,, constructing or projected

THE FIGURES REFER TO THE BOUNDARY TREATIES AND OTHER DOCUMENTS CONTAINED IN THE BODY OF THE WORK.
The Boundaries shewn on this Map are approximately correct, but should not be consulted as regards detail.

Du Bois (*second from right*) was among the speakers at the Second Pan-African Congress held in Europe in 1921. At the Congress, Du Bois said that although Africa was behind other nations in economic and social development it did not mean that Africans were inferior or that members of industrialized nations were superior. Rather, the gap was "proof of the essential richness and variety of human nature. . . ."

Black peoples in the African colonies mined gold and diamonds and harvested coffee beans, cocoa beans, and rubber from rubber trees. The materials and the money that they yielded went back to the white peoples of Europe. Du Bois believed that the situation was unfair, and that black Africans faced similar injustices as those encountered by African Americans. Although many African Americans worked long, hard hours on farms and in factories, they remained poor, while the white owners of the farms and of the factories became rich.

Du Bois began to address the problem after he attended the first Pan-African Congress in London in 1900. The Pan-African movement had been organized with the goal of securing rights and liberties for Africans around the world. Additional conferences were held in 1919, 1921, 1923, and 1927. The movement called for black Africans to "participate in the Government as fast as their development permits." This was not a radical message, as it labeled the black African colonies as undeveloped and not yet able to govern themselves. However, it was a call for change that acknowledged that the black peoples who made up a majority of the world's population should be involved in their government. Through education and opportunity, black Africans could ensure that their government operated on their behalf.

At this first Pan-African conference, W.E.B. Du Bois made his prophetic statement, "The problem of the Twentieth Century is the problem of the color-line." Du Bois was right. The struggles for independence in Africa and civil rights in the United States were major events that brought about immense change in the twentieth century.

6. Booker T. Washington and the Niagara Conference

Booker T. Washington was the most recognized black educator and leader from the end of Reconstruction in 1877 until his death in 1915. Born in 1856, Washington had been a slave on a tobacco farm in Virginia. After slaves were freed, he moved with his family to work in the coal mines of West Virginia. He received an education at Hampton Institute and then stayed on at Hampton as a teacher.

In 1881, Washington founded the Tuskegee Normal and Industrial Institute in Alabama. The school specialized in industrial education, which meant students were trained to become carpenters, builders, farmers, and barbers. The courses at Tuskegee did not focus on the type of material that Du Bois himself had studied, such as history, culture, art, and economics. Many people, both white and black, saw industrial education as a way to a more promising future for poor black people because it provided training that would help blacks to find jobs.

This 1903 photograph of Booker T. Washington, founder of the Tuskegee Normal and Industrial Institute, was taken by the Cheynes Studio. In order to learn skills that would help them to gain employment after graduation, Tuskegee students grew much of their food and constructed buildings for the campus. This practice allowed Washington to run the school on a limited budget.

Washington was remarkably successful at promoting his school and its ideals. His status as a spokesman for blacks increased after a speech he made at the 1895 Cotton States and International Exposition in Atlanta, Georgia. Later the speech became known as the Atlanta Compromise. Washington argued that whites should allow blacks to progress slowly in business and farming. In exchange, blacks would put off until later their demands for the right to vote and an end to segregation.

There was opposition to Booker T. Washington's idea that the fight for civil rights should be temporarily halted. Ida Wells-Barnett, a teacher and journalist, and William Monroe Trotter, the editor of the Boston *Guardian* and a Harvard classmate of Du Bois's, led the resistance movement against Washington's ideas. As quickly as possible, these black leaders wanted the right to vote and an end to the violence and discrimination against African Americans. Their call for immediate action gained momentum over time.

In 1903, Du Bois laid out his arguments against the

I. Garland Penn sketched Ida Wells-Barnett in 1891. When a train conductor ordered Wells-Barnett to give up her seat to a white man in 1884, she refused. She was dragged from the car by two men.

In 1892, Ida Wells-Barnett began a campaign against lynching after three of her friends were lynched by a mob in Memphis, Tennessee. As a journalist, she investigated the pasts of a large group of black people who had been lynched. Wells-Barnett did this by reviewing records and talking to people who had known the victims.

She found that many of these black people had not committed any crimes and had been killed unjustly. Ida Wells-Barnett's work destroyed the widespread theory of the time that only black criminals were lynched. She proved that many African Americans who were tortured and hanged by angry mobs were innocent.

As a result of her efforts, Wells-Barnett was forced out of Memphis by a mob. However, her campaign brought an international awareness to the problem of illegal mob lynching.

Atlanta Compromise and in favor of blacks demanding both the vote and an end to segregation in the essay "Of Mr. Booker T. Washington and Others." This essay was published in *The Souls of Black Folk*. Washington's influential supporters soon fought back. They made it clear to Atlanta University that the administrators should control W.E.B. Du Bois. If the administration failed to do so, Washington's supporters would no longer contribute money to the school.

Although a growing number of blacks disapproved of Washington's plan for achieving economic success first and political rights second, there was no nationwide black organization to fight for the civil rights of African Americans. Du Bois proposed that highly educated African Americans, such as Trotter, Wells-Barnett, and himself, would have to lead the fight. He called this group of African American doctors, newspaper publishers, teachers, and preachers the Talented Tenth.

W.E.B. Du Bois is often criticized for his idea that only the educated elite could be leaders in the fight for civil rights. His Talented Tenth concept ignored the strong African American communities across the United States that were composed of ordinary people who could also lead in the fight for equality.

In 1905, Du Bois organized a conference to discuss aggressive action by individuals "who believe in Negro freedom and growth." Twenty-nine respected black leaders from about fourteen states showed up for the small gathering. The meeting was called the Niagara Conference because it was held on the Canadian side of the Niagara Falls. The result of the meeting was a bold manifesto called the Declaration of Principles that demanded freedom of speech and press, the right to vote for all, the abolition of segregation, the right to earn a living, the right to an education, and a united leadership to realize these ideals. This small group of black leaders, guided by the

Some attendees of the 1905 Niagara Conference posed for a picture in front of Niagara Falls. Booker T. Washington exerted his influence with the press to ensure that there was little coverage in U.S. newspapers of this important meeting.

Declaration of Principles, was the basis for what became known as the Niagara Movement.

The need to press for immediate civil-rights reform was made even clearer by the 1906 racial riot in Atlanta, Georgia. A mob of as many as ten thousand poor, angry, young white men began attacking any black person they found on the streets. The riot was a

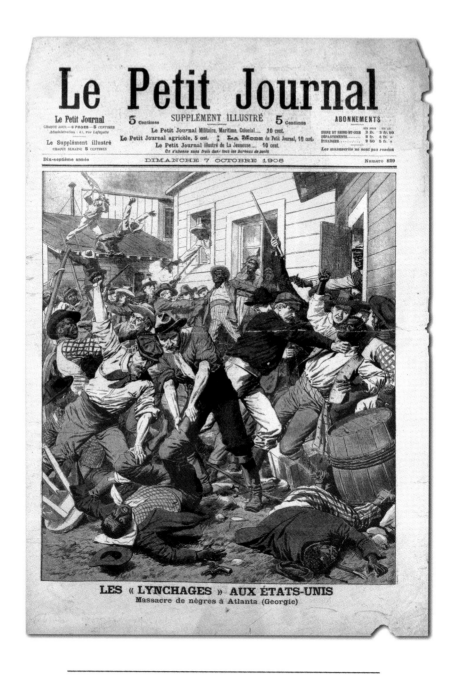

The 1906 Atlanta Race Riot was depicted in the French publication "Le Petit Journal" on October 7, 1906. Walter White, who witnessed the riot when he was thirteen, later described the horror in his 1948 memoir: "I was glad I was not one of those who hated; I was glad I was not one of those made sick and murderous by pride."

response to newspaper articles that reported that the number of black men who attacked white women was increasing. By the time that the riots ended, an estimated twelve black people and four or five white people had been killed in the fighting. Many more black people had been beaten and injured by angry white mobs.

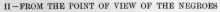

II—FROM THE POINT OF VIEW OF THE NEGROES

BY

W. E. BURGHARDT DU BOIS

AUTHOR OF "THE SOULS OF BLACK FOLK"

> 4. The Negro must have the ballot. Only in this way can he peacefully defend his life and property, help the best class of whites defend theirs and put down the criminals of both races.

W.E.B. Du Bois reported on the Atlanta race riot in this November 1906 editorial published in the *World Today*. Du Bois wrote that only by securing the vote could blacks be protected from racial violence.

Despite the great need for civil-rights reform, the Niagara Movement did not last. Members of the organization often disagreed on the direction the group should take. The strong personalities of Du Bois and Trotter clashed. Du Bois, the famous professor and author, was a scholar. Trotter, the editor, was more of an agitator. Trotter wanted to be more radical in the fight for civil rights. Du Bois, on the other hand, was concerned with winning the most followers, both white and black. In addition, Du Bois was not a politician who "could slap people on the back and make friends of strangers." Du Bois admitted, "I was no natural leader of men."

7. The NAACP and the *Crisis* Years

The National Association for the Advancement of Colored People (NAACP) was founded in 1909. The group was organized in response to an outburst of racial rioting and violence in Springfield, Illinois. Concerned white men and women from the Northeast, such as William English Walling, a reporter, Mary Ovington, a New York social reformer and activist, and Oswald Garrison Villard, editor of the New York *Evening Post*, were among the organization's founders.

Du Bois joined the NAACP as the group's first African American member because the Niagara Movement was losing its momentum. Ida Wells-Barnett and William Monroe Trotter refused to join an organization with white leadership. They were insulted also that they had not been selected to serve on the Committee of Forty. This group would create the organization's framework and then select the people who would run the NAACP as well. Despite this initial lack of support from African American leaders, the NAACP would become the most powerful civil rights organization in the United States.

Du Bois resigned his teaching position at Atlanta University to accept a full-time job with the NAACP as the director of publications and research. As Du Bois saw it, his career as a social scientist was replaced by a career in civil rights propaganda. He moved to New York and his family soon joined him there. Perhaps the most important part of this position was that Du Bois became the founding editor of *The Crisis: A Record of the Darker Races*.

The *Crisis* was a monthly journal for African Americans. The publication carried news of the civil rights movement, and, according to Du Bois, "placed clearly and consistently before the country a clear-cut statement of the legitimate aims of the American Negro."

The *Crisis* was first published in 1910 with a print run of 1,000 copies. At the height of the journal's popularity, more than 100,000 copies were often printed. This was the paper that African Americans read and trusted the most. Du Bois's own research and thoughts from 1910 until 1934 were presented within the pages of the *Crisis*. The publication was Du Bois's idea, and, even though the *Crisis* was associated with the NAACP, Du Bois managed the publication almost independently from that organization. Although Du Bois preferred this editorial independence, the practice

---

Next spread: W.E.B. Du Bois (*standing at far right*) and other staff members of *The Crisis: A Record of the Darker Races* are shown working in the publication's headquarters in New York around 1911.

THE CRISIS

A RECORD OF THE DARKER RACES

Volume One	DECEMBER, 1910	Number Two

Edited by W. E. BURGHARDT DU BOIS, with the co-operation of Oswald Garrison Villard, J. Max Barber, Charles Edward Russell, Kelly Miller, W. S. Braithwaite and M. D. Maclean.

This magazine is the organ of the National Association for the advancement of Colored People, upon whose General Committee are persons like Moorfield Storey, Professor Seligman, Anna Garlin Spencer, Francis J. Garrison, Jacob Schiff, President Charles Thwing, Jane Addams, Mary Church Terrell, Judge Stafford, and others.

The periodical will be edited by W. E. Burghardt DuBois, director of Publicity and Research in this organization. Associated with Dr. DuBois in the conduct of the magazine will be the following persons:

Oswald Garrison Villard, assistant editor of the New York *Evening Post*.

Charles Edward Russell, the well-known magazine writer.

Kelly Miller, Dean of the College Department of Howard University and an author and critic.

J. Max Barber, formerly editor of the *Voice of the Negro*.

William Stanley Braithwaite, a poet and writer of international reputation.

Mrs. Dunlop Maclean, a staff writer on the New York *Times*.

Besides these writers, contributors will embrace some of the best-known names in America and the world.

The magazine will be small but carefully edited.

The December number contains 36 pages, illustrated, and reaches 10,000 readers among philanthropists, students and educated colored people.

PUBLISHED MONTHLY BY THE

National Association for the Advancement of Colored People

AT TWENTY VESEY STREET   NEW YORK CITY

ONE DOLLAR A YEAR   TEN CENTS A COPY

(OVER)

This is the December 1910 cover of the *Crisis*. When Du Bois launched the journal in 1910, he stated that the publication's mission was to present "those facts and arguments which show the danger of race prejudice." The print run, or the number of copies that were printed, for this December issue was 2,500.

often caused conflict with the leadership of the NAACP, as the *Crisis* did not always reflect the views of the NAACP in print.

The influence of the NAACP grew after the death of Booker T. Washington in 1915. The conservative portion of the civil rights movement had lost their leader. Du Bois had respected Washington's accomplishments, but he believed it was time for more aggressive action to end the violence and discrimination toward blacks.

As the NAACP rose in importance for African Americans, the world plunged into the horrors of World War I. This war, which lasted from 1914 to 1918, was fought to obtain territory and political domination, and it aligned the European nations against one another. World War I started in Europe in 1914, and the United States entered the conflict in 1917. The *Crisis* reported on the conflict for the African American community.

At first the U.S. government did not want African American volunteers in the military. Then a law was passed that allowed for segregated army units. Most African American units served as laborers and servants. Some black men served as soldiers, although in smaller numbers.

Du Bois argued against a segregated army, but the U.S. Army would not allow blacks and whites to fight alongside one another. The NAACP was, however, able to secure training for African Americans to become officers.

Abraham Lincoln is shown looking down upon a group of African American soldiers battling German soldiers in this World War I poster entitled *True Sons of Freedom*. Gustrine Chas created this poster in 1918.

They could only lead segregated army units. By 1917, there were about six hundred African Americans who had received commissions as officers.

During the summer of 1917, racial violence broke out in Houston, Texas, and St. Louis, Missouri. Despite these outbreaks of violence against blacks, Du Bois wrote a 1918 editorial for the *Crisis* called "Close Ranks." In his editorial Du Bois wrote, "Let us, while this war lasts, forget our special grievances and close our ranks shoulder to shoulder with our white fellow citizens and allied nations that are fighting for democracy."

Some African American leaders criticized Du Bois for his article. They argued that it was the ideal time for action. Du Bois's call to put differences aside seemed similar to the views of Booker T. Washington, against which Du Bois himself had argued for so many years. What the readers of the *Crisis* did not know was that the federal government was applying pressure to the NAACP to lessen its criticism of the government.

Du Bois and others believed that if African Americans fought bravely, they would earn respect and be rewarded for their contribution to America. More than 350,000 African American men fought in World War I, in which the United States and its allies defeated Germany and its allies.

Du Bois celebrated the soldiers' homecoming with a 1919 *Crisis* editorial called "Returning Soldiers." In this essay Du Bois declared that the brave black soldiers were returning to a nation filled with prejudice. He said that the United States, "despite all its better souls have done and dreamed, is yet a shameful land . . . Make way for Democracy! We saved it in France, and by the Great Jehovah, we will save it in the United States of America, or know the reason why."

Despite Du Bois's hopes that the contributions of African American soldiers would bring improvements for all African Americans, after fighting for their country in World War I, African American soldiers came back to a segregated nation and hatred by whites. Another wave of racial violence swept across the country in 1919, when African American soldiers returned home. More than seventy black men and women were lynched in the Deep South in 1919, and more than two hundred and fifty were killed in race riots in Northern cities.

During this turbulent time, Du Bois was sent to Europe at the end of 1918. Thanks to his roles in the NAACP and the Pan-African movement, he was asked to participate in the Versailles Peace Conference held in France. This conference resulted in the Treaty of Versailles, which officially ended World War I. Du Bois was invited to give advice on the creation of the League of Nations, a forerunner to the United Nations. During his stay in Europe, Du Bois spent some time organizing future Pan-African conferences.

While Du Bois was abroad, a radical movement for black nationalism was gaining popularity in the United

The Signing of Peace in the Hall of Mirrors, Versailles, 28th June 1919 was painted by Sir William Orpen in the early 1920s. The artist dramatized the Versailles Peace Conference, which resulted in a treaty that officially ended WWI. The French king Louis XIV, who lived until 1715, made additions to his palace at Versailles, including the Hall of Mirrors.

Marcus Garvey, shown in a 1923 photograph, encouraged African Americans to be proud of their cultural identity. He advised black parents to promote this confidence by giving "children dolls that look like them to play with and cuddle."

States. Black nationalism is the idea that black people should be economically, socially, and politically independent in order to gain equality in a society that favors whites. Marcus Garvey was a leader of the black nationalism movement. During the 1920s, Garvey gave impassioned speeches on behalf of the civil rights movement.

Marcus Garvey was born on August 17, 1887, in Jamaica. He went to school until he was fourteen and then worked as a printer. Garvey spent time traveling and observing the social conditions of blacks in Central America before attending college in London.

Garvey moved to the United States in 1916, during the race riots in St. Louis and Houston. He settled in the Harlem neighborhood of New York City and organized the Universal Negro Improvement Association

(UNIA). Garvey's message that blacks should be self-reliant struck a chord with many African Americans. With help from UNIA, and to promote his goal of black economic independence, Garvey started his own shipping business. New black immigrants from the Caribbean Islands of the West Indies were particularly impressed by Garvey's achievement. These immigrants were often poor and were looked down upon by other African Americans. Garvey also supported a Back to Africa movement. The movement called for black peoples across the world to move to Africa, which was to be controlled by black people.

As UNIA grew in popularity, so did criticism of it by Du Bois and other African American leaders. Garvey countered by attacking Du Bois's position in the "Close Ranks" essay. He also criticized the NAACP and Du Bois for being elitist and unrepresentative of the black West Indian immigrants.

However, Garvey took his separatism too far. He met with a white supremacist Ku Klux Klan leader in an effort to gain white people's support for the Back to Africa movement. Du Bois as well as many of Garvey's supporters thought this was a terrible choice. Garvey's influence was greatly reduced by both his meeting with the Ku Klux Klan and the shady financing of his shipping business. Garvey was arrested in 1923 for financial misdealings. In 1927 he was deported from, or forced to leave, the United States. Marcus Garvey did not return to America or regain his former fame. He continued to write and publish until his death in London in 1940.

Garvey's message of black self-reliance did have a lasting impact on African Americans. In the 1920s, the African American community developed an intense awareness of its own culture and history. An offshoot of this self-reflection was a growth of African American creativity that resulted in new works of fiction, poetry, and jazz. This movement by African American artists

William H. Johnson, a Harlem Renaissance painter, created *Street Life, Harlem* around 1940. Johnson studied art in the United States and in Europe. In the late 1930s, he was hired to teach an art class at the Harlem Community Art Center.

The 1928 wedding in Harlem of Du Bois's daughter Nina Yolande to the writer Countee Cullen was a major social event. Nina Yolande insisted on having a large wedding and there were sixteen bridesmaids in her bridal party. She is at the center of the image with a long veil.

became known as the Harlem Renaissance. The *Crisis* encouraged this movement by selecting beautiful images and pictures by black artists for its covers and by publishing works of poetry and fiction by black authors.

Du Bois also made a special effort for African American children. In 1920, he began publication of a short-lived monthly magazine for children called *The Brownie's Book*. The magazine was designed to make African American children proud of who they were and to teach them about African American history and current events.

8. Depression and Action

The Harlem Renaissance was part of the overall good fortune that the United States enjoyed in the 1920s. The economy was growing, and people had jobs and regular paychecks. This good fortune ended in October 1929, with the crash of the stock market. The once-healthy U.S. economy slowed down and sank into a fiscal depression. Companies sold fewer products and went out of business or fired many employees in hopes of operating with much smaller staffs. Many people lost their jobs and had no money to spend on food or shelter.

The Great Depression, as it was known, took a heavy toll on African Americans. Many working black people, most of whom had little or no savings, lost their jobs. Additionally, the farms, homes, and savings of many middle-class black people, who had made some gains in the 1920s, were lost. In 1929, the *Crisis* itself faced bankruptcy because readers of the magazine could no longer afford to buy the publication. Only financial support from the NAACP kept the *Crisis* from ruin.

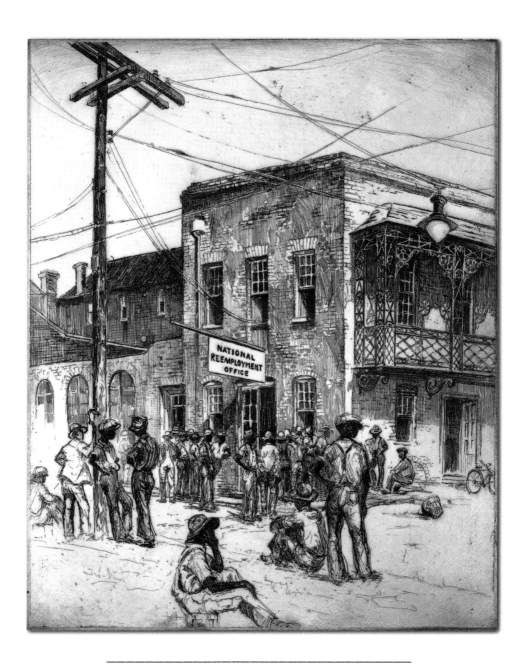

This etching by Elizabeth O'Neill Verner from around 1930 depicts the unemployed in Charleston, South Carolina. When U.S. companies faced financial difficulties in the 1930s, African American employees were usually fired first. Therefore, many blacks were unemployed longer than were whites during the Great Depression.

During the Great Depression, W.E.B. Du Bois explored the idea that socialism would help end some of the world's evils. Socialism is an economic system that is based on cooperation rather than competition. An economic system is simply the way people acquire goods. Goods can mean food, medical care, school, aid to the unemployed, and assistance for the elderly. The goal of socialism is the fair allocation of goods. In socialism the government plays a big role in allocating, or distributing, goods more equally.

America has an economic system called capitalism. Capitalism allows individuals and companies to compete for goods. Under this type of system, a free market should determine the price of goods. Although the government does not play a strong role in setting the price, it does make sure that markets are fair and that no one corporation has a monopoly, or complete power over an industry. Capitalism has contributed to America's rank as a world power and has made some Americans wealthy. However, many Americans remain poor.

Socialism and capitalism are not opposites. There are varying degrees to each economic system. Hard choices have to be made and there are no right answers. Which goods should the government pay for? Which goods should citizens pay for? If people or companies earn a great deal of money, how much should they be allowed to keep, and how much should they contribute in taxes? If taxes are high, will people and

Sweden is often considered a socialist country. In Sweden people pay the government a great deal in taxes but have more access to healthcare and education. Although the United States is a capitalist country, there are social programs such as social security to provide financial aid to senior citizens and the disabled. Workers pay a payroll tax to fund this U.S. program.

companies continue to work hard? How does a government ensure that all citizens obtain a good education and quality healthcare?

Du Bois saw how the Great Depression damaged the fortunes of African Americans. Increasingly, he turned to the idea of socialism as a way to reduce the gaps between the very rich and the very poor by giving more people an opportunity to succeed.

One way Du Bois tried to promote socialist ideals was to suggest that black leaders focus on "planning for the future of the Negro economy, for solving the question as to how the Negro is going to earn a decent living."

Du Bois's plan called for African American leaders to strategize for an economy that made sure that African Americans could earn a decent wage. Du Bois thought that by working together as a community to start companies, give one another jobs, and spend money within the community, African Americans could raise themselves out of the Depression.

Du Bois's proposal that African Americans plan their own economy and work together was considered a form of voluntary segregation. This went against the views of the NAACP, who demanded a united voice on behalf of African Americans. The growing NAACP was working hard to end segregation, particularly in schools. Du Bois was often at odds with Walter White, who headed the NAACP at the time.

In 1934, Du Bois was forced to give up editorial control of the *Crisis*. "To give up *The Crisis* was like giving up a child," Du Bois later recalled. Du Bois had lost one of his platforms for communicating with the African American community. He resigned from the NAACP in protest.

Du Bois returned to Atlanta University as the head of the

Walter White, photographed around 1930, helped block the appointment of Judge John J. Parker to the U.S. Supreme Court. Parker was against black suffrage.

sociology department. In the next decade he focused his energy on his writing. Over the next ten years, Du Bois published four books and had numerous articles printed in various magazines.

Du Bois's history of Reconstruction, called *Black Reconstruction in America*, was published in 1935. Reconstruction was the period following the Civil War, from 1865 to 1877, which set the conditions whereby the southern states could be allowed to return to the Union. The South was put under military control. The southern states were required to ratify the Thirteenth and Fourteenth Amendments to the U.S. Constitution. These amendments outlawed slavery and guaranteed full political and civil rights to African Americans.

In *Black Reconstruction in America*, Du Bois detailed the successes and failures of Reconstruction. He used scientific historical analysis to show the gains that African Americans had made in terms of income and political power under Reconstruction. In particular, he highlighted the successes of the Freedmen's Bureau, which was often seen as a failure for not delivering the promised "40 acres [16 ha] and a mule" to every African American. Despite the bureau's many failures, Du Bois showed how the Freedmen's Bureau did help many African Americans to make the transition from slavery to freedom by setting up schools and helping the former slaves to become farmers, workers, and leaders in local government.

The Freedmen's Bureau funded educational programs for emancipated African Americans. James E. Taylor's 1866 engraving documented industrial training in sewing for some women in Richmond, Virginia.

Black Reconstruction showed what African Americans could achieve if they were given the opportunity. The book also documented the devastating impact that the end of Reconstruction had on African Americans. Du Bois's conclusion was that the rise of the white South, Jim Crow laws, and discrimination had set African Americans back almost a century.

In *Dusk of Dawn: An Essay Toward an Autobiography of a Race Concept*, W.E.B. Du Bois wrote about the quest for freedom of black peoples across the globe. This book reflected his growing frustration with the pace of change in the fight for civil rights, the economic depression, and the continued violence toward African Americans.

In 1940, W.E.B. Du Bois founded and edited a magazine called *Phylon*. The magazine was published quarterly and explored the issue of race relations through subjects such as literature, history, and social sciences.

Atlanta University forced Du Bois into retirement in 1944 when the university failed to renew his contract. University officials worried that Du Bois's political views might reflect poorly on Atlanta University and that the school would lose funding from donors. Du Bois protested, but without success. "I found myself at the age of 76 without employment and less than $5,000 of savings," Du Bois recalled.

Du Bois was offered several jobs and soon accepted an offer from the NAACP. Although Du Bois did not really want to work with NAACP leader Walter White again, the job offer was promising. He became the director of special research and moved back to New York. However, what Du Bois thought his job entailed and what the NAACP wanted him to do were two different things. Du Bois thought he was hired to offer his opinion on specific issues when asked but mostly to research the role of the NAACP in Africa.

What actually happened was that Du Bois served as White's writer and as an NAACP representative. According to Du Bois the NAACP wanted him to "willingly act as window dressing, say a proper word now and then and give the Association and its secretary moral support." Du Bois was still a famous African American leader. Despite Du Bois's recent radical views, the NAACP wanted to benefit from his fame.

Increasingly it became clear that Du Bois and White could not work together. Du Bois was a famous individual who had his own opinions on the issues of the day. These opinions would sometimes be different than the official view held by the NAACP.

For example, Du Bois was openly critical of the United Nations, because the organization refused to take a stand against colonialism. The NAACP did not want to criticize the United Nations. The NAACP saw the United Nations as an organization that might aid the NAACP in the fight to end racial segregation in the United States.

Walter White was frustrated that he could not control what Du Bois said and did. For his part, Du Bois was also frustrated. In the fall of 1948, he wrote a memo to the NAACP board of directors that was critical of White. The memo was leaked to the newspapers shortly after it was written, and it became a big story. Du Bois claimed that he did not leak the memo, and he probably did not. However, at the end of 1948, Du Bois was fired from the NAACP.

9. A Communist in the Cold War

The pace and scope of reform that William Edward Burghardt Du Bois demanded was too great for the NAACP. The problem of race was a global issue for Du Bois, and he was looking for a global solution to the problem. After Du Bois left the NAACP in 1948, he turned increasingly to more radical forms of socialism, such as communism, as an answer to the issues faced by black peoples.

Communism is a more extreme form of socialism in which all people are equal and the government controls public services and most aspects of society. Du Bois was attracted to these ideas because of the equality and opportunity communism promised at a time when black people were not treated equally or given many opportunities to succeed. Du Bois's political views took him far away from mainstream American politics and also well outside the views of most African Americans.

Du Bois was inspired by the reported social progress that had been achieved by Communist Russia, or the Union of Soviet Socialist Republics (U.S.S.R.).

As W.E.B. Du Bois advanced in his life and studies, he began to embrace the ideals of communism. Communism is considered to be an ideology, or a collection of ideas, which is the opposite of capitalism.

In a Communist society, there is no individual ownership of goods. The community, not the individual, owns property, such as factories, apartments, farms, and hospitals.

The government oversees the distribution of community property. In theory, all people have equal access to food, housing, schools, and healthcare.

Additionally, Du Bois respected the Soviet Union for supporting Africa's attempt to fight colonization. Du Bois visited the Soviet Union first in 1926, and again in 1936, 1949, and 1958. Du Bois also visited China in 1936 and again in 1959.

During these visits, Communist governmental officials took Du Bois around their country to view their best schools, factories, and hospitals. To Du Bois it appeared that the new governments had problems but worked to provide equality to all people, both men and women alike. The Communist governments sought to provide equal access to healthcare and to decrease the rates of illiteracy by making schooling available to all citizens. Before

W.E.B. Du Bois was awarded the Soviet Union's Lenin Peace Prize in 1958. This medal recognized his contributions to world peace. Vladimir Ilich Lenin was one of the principal leaders behind the revolution in Russia that eventually led to the formation of the Soviet Union.

the Communist governments had been installed, leaders who were similar to kings had ruled both Russia and China. These leaders had been exceptionally wealthy, while many of the people in these countries had been poor and hungry.

Du Bois admitted that living conditions in the Soviet Union and China were still below those of middle-class America, but he pointed out that many more people were able to vote, go to school, and earn a living. For Du Bois, the potential benefits of communism for poor black people seemed clear.

However, Du Bois refused to recognize the consequences and the high price people paid for communism in Russia and China. The reality was that millions of people died under communism in these two countries, often from starvation. The governments sold much of the food their citizens produced to other countries in order to raise money to build factories, weapons, and other industrial projects. Although the Soviet Union and China held elections, the elections were often false, and often one dictator controlled the entire country. People who disagreed with the government were killed or sent to prison camps because they expressed differing political beliefs.

Du Bois probably knew about these serious problems because they were reported in U.S. newspapers. However, Du Bois viewed these problems as part of a painful growth process that was necessary to build a new society. He also defended these governments' political oppression as being less harmful than the oppression and murder of black people in the United States and Africa. Du Bois was more familiar with the serious problems of the United States because he experienced racial discrimination firsthand and saw the poverty that many African Americans endured.

The United States and the Soviet Union had been allies during World War II. After the war, however, they quickly became competitors and enemies. They clashed because of their different political and economic systems. The United States functioned under a capitalist government, and the Soviet Union operated under a Communist one. The result of this clash was an intense, dangerous competition between the two most powerful countries in the world. This fierce rivalry was called the cold war. Although no wars were fought between the two countries during the cold war period between 1945 and 1989, tensions ran high. Both countries had nuclear weapons and large armies and were capable of destroying each other. During the cold war, people experienced a constant fear of nuclear war. In the United States there were also intense anti-Communist feelings.

The U.S. government quickly decided that anything that was Communist was also anti-American because of its conflict with the Soviet Union. A moblike atmosphere gripped the United States as the nation searched to root out anything and anyone considered Communist. Congress set up the House Un-American Activities Committee (HUAC) and began to investigate any individual they suspected of being a Communist. Du Bois was defiant in both his support of communism and his defense of the Soviet Union. This would increasingly put him at odds with the U.S. government and the many African Americans who supported the U.S. government during the cold war.

Du Bois soon became involved in the international movement for peace and a ban on nuclear weapons. In 1949, Du Bois helped to organize the Cultural and Scientific Conference for World Peace in New York City.

This photograph was taken on October 21, 1947. Representative
J. Parnell Thomas (*left*), chairman of the House Un-American Activities
Committee, is being sworn in before testifying to the committee. Most
witnesses were asked if they were Communists. Witnesses were also
asked to name other people whom they knew to be Communists.

He also attended peace conferences in Paris, France, and Moscow, U.S.S.R. Because of the anti-Communist fervor in the United States, Du Bois was the only American to attend the conference in Moscow.

As Du Bois was beginning his crusade for peace, his wife, Nina Gomer Du Bois, died. She passed away in Baltimore, Maryland, in July 1950, and was buried in Great Barrington. She had been Du Bois's loyal wife for 54 years, although the marriage had not always been a happy one. The death of their son Burghardt and Du Bois's hectic work and travel schedule had affected the couple's relationship.

Du Bois dealt with Nina's death by focusing on his work. In 1951, he also found consolation when he married Shirley Graham. Du Bois said that his longtime friend Graham "finally persuaded herself that I needed her help and companionship, as I certainly did." Shirley Graham was a teacher, a writer, and a political activist, who first met Du Bois in 1920. In 1936, the two began talking to each other more frequently and

Shirley Graham and W.E.B. Du Bois were photographed together on February 23, 1955, on Du Bois's eighty-seventh birthday. In his *Autobiography*, Du Bois wrote of his second wife, "She was a woman 40 years my junior but her work and aim in life had been close to mine . . . She has made these days [of my life] rich and rewarding."

their relationship deepened. The couple got along quite well because they shared many of the same ideas on civil rights and socialism. In 1946, Shirley Graham had introduced Du Bois to some other notable Americans who believed in communism, such as the African American actor Paul Robeson and the writer Howard Fast.

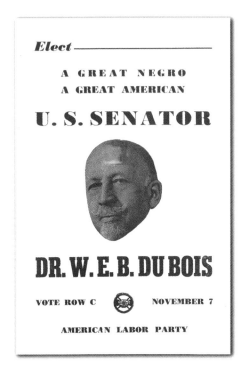

Elect——————

A GREAT NEGRO
A GREAT AMERICAN

U. S. SENATOR

DR. W. E. B. DU BOIS

VOTE ROW C   NOVEMBER 7

AMERICAN LABOR PARTY

This campaign flyer promoted the candidacy of W.E.B. Du Bois to the U.S. Senate in 1950. He ran for office on the American Labor Party's election ticket.

Du Bois became the chairman of the Peace Information Center in 1950. The goals of the center were to inform Americans of the various peace movements around the world and to gather signatures for a petition in support of the Stockholm Peace Appeal for a nuclear weapons ban.

With Du Bois, Robeson, Shirley Graham, and other American communists involved in the Peace Information Center, it did not take long for the government to attack the center as a Communist organization. In July 1950, U.S. Secretary of State Dean Acheson called the "world peace appeal" or "Stockholm resolution" a "propaganda trick" put on by the Soviet Union. Du Bois replied to Acheson's comments soon after by writing, "Does it not occur to you, Sir, that there are honest Americans who, Regardless of their differences on other questions, hate and fear war and are determined to do something to avert it?"

During this same time in 1950, when he was 82 years old, Du Bois was approached by the American Labor Party to run for the U.S. Senate as a candidate from New York. The American Labor Party was a small political party that fought for the rights of workers and a more socialist economy that would narrow the gap between rich people and poor people.

Du Bois was not a politician and knew he had little chance of winning. On the other hand, the campaign allowed him to speak on behalf of world peace. His name recognition would also help the congressional campaign of Labor candidate Vito Marcantonio. "I went into the campaign for Senator knowing well from

Vito Marcantonio, shown in 1941, was a U.S. Congressman for 14 years. He believed that the Communist Party was simply another political party, one that served the "interests of the American working class and people."

[Enc.]

This appeal was issued at Stockholm in March, 1950 by the World Committee in Defense of Peace.

TRYGVE LIE, Secretary of the United Nations, said of this Committee:

"I bless everyone, every man and woman, who works for peace."

INTERNATIONAL RED CROSS:

"The A-bomb means total destruction . . . ban it."

THOMAS MANN, Writer, Nobel Prize Winner:

"I have signed the Stockholm appeal. I support any movement which has peace as its aim."

WM. HOOD, Recording Sec'y, Ford Local 600, UAW, CIO:

"I am for world peace. If we don't have peace we won't be around to struggle for more democracy and better working conditions."

ABBE BOULIER, French Catholic Leader:

"God does not want the atomic bomb dropped on . . . any capital. All peoples should adhere to our appeal, adopted in Stockholm, which condemns any employment of the atomic weapon and brands as criminal that government which first uses it. We hope that other organizations fighting for peace will join us."

24-24-33

Thruout the world—
In China, Italy, Israel, in England and Brazil, in France and Mexico, in Finland and Poland, Sweden and the Soviet Union, in Africa and India and in the United States—
Tens of millions of people of all faiths and creeds, all races are signing this appeal.
If we, the people say NO to war
THERE WILL BE PEACE

WORLD PEACE APPEAL

● We demand the outlawing of atomic weapons as instruments of intimidation and mass murder of peoples. We demand strict international control to enforce this measure.

● We believe that any government which first uses atomic weapons against any other country whatsoever will be committing a crime against humanity and should be dealt with as a war criminal.

● We call on all men and women of good will thruout the world to sign this appeal.

Name	City
Minnie Heller	Oralill Ind
Kurt Gartner	Fort - Wayne Ind
Mm Gertrude Gartner	Ft Wayne Ind
Harvey Gunter	Ft Wayne Ind
Norval E. Jameson	Ft Wayne Ind.
Grace Kitt	Fort Wayne, Ind
Dorothy Jamieson	Fort Wayne, Ind.
Frances Hart	Fort Wayne Ind
Iola McCague	Ft. Wayne Ind
Bessie E. Fisher	West Unity Ohio
Louella Austin	Bryant Ohio

Return this petition to:

Collected by........................... Address...........................

Made available by: PEACE INFORMATION CENTER
P. O. Box 349, Grand Central Station, New York City

N° 405627

The Peace Information Center collected signatures on behalf of Stockholm Peace Appeal, a worldwide petition that sought to ban nuclear weapons. This particular petition was circulated in Indiana and Ohio in 1950. By July 13, 1950, the Peace Information Center had collected about 1.5 million signatures in the United States.

the first that I did not have a ghost of a chance for election. . . .” Du Bois lost the election, but made a respectable showing as 205,729 people voted for him.

The election campaign did not stop the U.S. government from pursuing the Peace Information Center. In August 1950, Du Bois received a telegram informing him that the Peace Information Center had to register as a foreign organization. The Peace Information Center replied that they were not going to register as they were an American organization, founded by and for Americans who were interested in peace.

In October, the Peace Information Center voted to disband. However, time was needed to close down the center's offices and its ongoing activities. The delay was not fast enough for the U.S. government. The federal government charged the Peace Information Center, Du Bois, and other Peace Information Center officials with the crime of refusing to register as an agent of foreign principal.

Many of Shirley Graham and Du Bois's friends expressed their support for Du Bois in his legal fight. The NAACP, however, offered no help. Walter White insisted that the Justice Department had evidence that the Soviet Union had supported the Peace Information Center. This was not true. The U.S. government had no evidence, and the judge dismissed the charges against Du Bois and the other defendants.

10. Final Years in Ghana

In 1952, the U.S. State Department would not reissue William Edward Burghardt Du Bois a U.S. passport for international travel. The State Department asked Du Bois to declare in writing that he was not a member of the Communist Party. "As a matter of fact, I was not a member of that party," Du Bois later said. However, at the time, he refused to make a statement, because "the government had no legal right to question me concerning my political beliefs."

Du Bois was issued a passport in 1958, when the Supreme Court decided that the U.S. State Department could not refuse U.S. citizens a passport because they refused to write down their political beliefs. Du Bois, his wife, Shirley, and their friends left for a long world tour in August 1958. "I felt like a released prisoner," Du Bois declared in his autobiography.

Du Bois toured Western Europe, the Soviet Union, and China. He met with Soviet leader Nikita Khrushchev in Moscow. In Beijing, China, Du Bois met with Chinese leader Mao Tse-tung. Du Bois's visit was a national

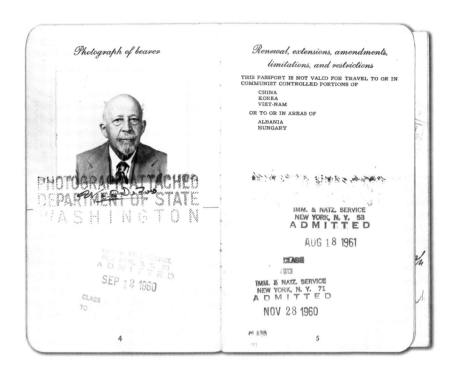

These pages from Du Bois's passport are stamped with dates of his reentry into New York City, New York, in 1960 and 1961, after Du Bois had traveled abroad. The passport specified that it was "not valid for travel to or in communist controlled portions of China, Korea, Viet-nam . . . Albania, Hungary."

event in China. In a speech Du Bois gave in China, he encouraged cooperation between China and the emerging black nations in Africa that formerly had been colonies. Du Bois felt that the tour was "one of the most important trips that I had ever taken, and had wide influence on my thought."

After he returned to the United States, Du Bois declared, "I believe in communism. I mean by communism, a planned way of life in the production of wealth and work designed for building a state whose object is

On W.E.B. Du Bois's February 1959 visit to China he was photographed with Chairman Mao Tse-tung. At the time of Du Bois's visit, political relations between the United States and the People's Republic of China were nonexistent. Americans had been ordered not to travel to Communist China.

the highest welfare of its people." In 1961, as a symbol of his beliefs, W.E.B. Du Bois became a member of the American Communist Party.

As Du Bois was focusing on the international peace movement and communism, the mainstream civil rights movement, which Du Bois had helped to launch, was gaining energy. In 1956, Du Bois gave his support to the Reverend Martin Luther King Jr. during the Montgomery bus boycott. The boycott arose when African Americans in Montgomery, Alabama, banned together and boycotted, or refused to ride, the local buses to protest segregation. Black passengers were

On December 1, 1955, Rosa Parks, an African American who lived in Montgomery, Alabama, refused to give up her seat on a bus to a white man. The photograph shows Parks being fingerprinted after her arrest for breaking Alabama's segregation laws. Parks sat down in the middle of the bus, where blacks were required to give up their seats to whites.

required to sit at the back of the bus and to give up their seats should a white passenger request them to do so.

Additionally, the NAACP, which had focused on fighting school segregation, was finally winning the battle in the federal courts. In 1954, the Supreme Court decided in the case of *Brown v. the Board of Education* that the segregation of schools for black and white children was unconstitutional.

Du Bois considered the decision to be monumental, "To me this success was beyond anything I had dreamed." With this praise came caution. Du Bois had lived through the end of Reconstruction, and **he** observed that although the court's decision was necessary, "it does not ensure action." He was right. Not until 1957, three years after the Supreme Court decision had been handed down, were schools in the South forced to begin integrating. This would only come about after President Eisenhower sent in the army to enforce integration in a Little Rock, Arkansas, high school.

Additionally, it was not until the Civil Rights Acts of 1964 and the Voting Rights Act of 1965 were passed, a decade after the Supreme Court decision, that African Americans were protected fully from discrimination and were given the right to vote. Before these acts were passed, black voters in some districts were restricted from voting because they could not pass a literacy test or were unable to pay a poll tax, a fee that was required before citizens were allowed to vote.

Change was happening also for black peoples abroad. In the 1950s and the 1960s, many African nations were gaining independence from European rulers. In 1960, W.E.B. Du Bois traveled to Ghana, a small country on the coast of West Africa, to participate in an independence celebration.

The next year, in 1961, Du Bois was invited to move to Ghana by Ghana's president, Kwame Nkrumah. Du Bois and his wife Shirley accepted the president's offer. Du Bois was still a hero to many Africans because he had

W.E.B. Du Bois and President Kwame Nkrumah of Ghana toast Du Bois's ninety-fifth birthday in February 1963. In March 1957, the nation of Ghana was established with Nkrumah as the country's first leader. In 1960, Ghana gained full independence and was no longer a part of the British Commonwealth. The British Commonwealth consists of nations and territories that are collectively associated with Britain.

been the driving force behind the Pan-African movement and had supported independence for black Africans.

Nkrumah thought that Du Bois's presence in Ghana would strengthen the reputation of his country. Du Bois could advise the leaders of Ghana and the other newly formed African countries on government and culture. Du Bois also had grand plans to direct a project called *Encyclopedia Africana*, which was designed to provide a comprehensive guide to the history and cultures of Africa.

After Du Bois became a member of the Communist Party and left the United States for Ghana, the U.S. government would neither renew his passport nor allow him to return. Therefore, W.E.B. Du Bois gave up his U.S. citizenship, and, in 1963, he became an official citizen of Ghana. W.E.B. Du Bois would never return to the United States.

In his ninety-fifth year of life, on August 27, 1963, Du Bois died quietly in Ghana's capital city, Accra. He died the day before the famous Civil Rights March on Washington, D.C. More than 200,000 people journeyed to the U.S. capital to demand equality for all U.S. citizens.

At the march, Roy Wilkins, the new head of the NAACP, announced to the crowd that Dr. Du Bois had died. Wilkins proclaimed, "Regardless of the fact that in his later years he chose a different path . . . his was the voice calling you to gather here today in this cause." Later that day, the Reverend Martin Luther King Jr.

Participants in the August 28, 1963, March on Washington were photographed in front of the Lincoln Memorial in Washington, D.C., for the *U.S. News and World Report*. Some of the protesters carried signs that said, "We March for Integrated Schools NOW!" and "We Demand Jobs for All NOW!"

would deliver his "I have a dream" speech, one of the most famous and moving speeches ever delivered. In this speech Reverend King said, "I have a dream that one day this nation will rise up and live out the true meaning of its creed: 'We hold these truths to be self-evident; that all men are created equal.'"

Du Bois was buried on August 29 in an elaborate state funeral. At a state funeral, representatives from foreign governments attend the burial of a distinguished person. Many governments from around the

Mourners gather around the casket of W.E.B. Du Bois at his state funeral held in Ghana in August 1963. Before his death Du Bois had prepared a speech that was to be read at his funeral by his wife Shirley, "I have loved my work . . . I have been uplifted by the thought that what I have done well will live long and justify my life."

world sent a representative to Du Bois's funeral. The United States did not send a representative. Du Bois's funeral celebrated his remarkable lifetime achievements in scholarship and activism. President Nkrumah of Ghana concluded his speech about Du Bois's accomplishments with, "Dr. Du Bois is a phenomenon. May he rest in peace."

William Edward Burghardt Du Bois challenged Americans to improve their society by giving African

Americans and the poor an equal opportunity. By the end of W.E.B. Du Bois's life, America had rejected him for his efforts. In his autobiography, Du Bois reflected wryly on his experiences in the United States. He wrote, "I would have been hailed with approval if I had died at 50. At 75 my death was practically requested."

Despite his decline in popularity in America and his troubles with the U.S. government late in his life, the impact and legacy of W.E.B. Du Bois is undeniable. During his life, he saw the worst injustices against African Americans since their enslavement before the Civil War. In response, he became a founder of the American civil rights movement. Du Bois was also recognized as the Father of Pan-Africanism for his efforts to ensure that the black peoples of Africa were free to govern themselves. W.E.B. Du Bois was a leading intellectual, social scientist, and writer whose works are still relevant and continue to be studied and used today.

Timeline

1868   William Edward Burghardt Du Bois is born on
            February 23 in Great Barrington, Massachusetts.

1880–1884   Du Bois attends Great Barrington High School. Du Bois
            also serves as the western Massachusetts correspondent
            for the New York *Globe* and the *Springfield Republican*.

1885–1888   Du Bois attends Fisk University in Nashville,
            Tennessee, and graduates in 1888. Du Bois teaches in a
            rural school district during the summer.

1888–1890   Du Bois earns an undergraduate degree from Harvard
            University.

1890–1892   Du Bois starts graduate studies at Harvard.

1892–1894   Du Bois earns a fellowship from the Slater Fund to
            study at the University of Berlin in Germany.

1894–1896   Du Bois teaches at Wilberforce University in Ohio.

1895   Du Bois earns a Ph.D. from Harvard.

1896   Nina Gomer and W.E.B. Du Bois are married on May 12.

            Du Bois's dissertation "The Suppression of the African
            Slave-Trade" is published.

1896–1897   Du Bois accepts a fellowship from the University of
            Pennsylvania to study a black community in
            Philadelphia. The result of his research, *The
            Philadelphia Negro*, is published in 1899.

1897–1910   Du Bois becomes a professor at Atlanta University in
            Georgia.

1903   *The Souls of Black Folk* is published.

1905	The Niagara Movement is founded to promote civil justice and abolish discrimination.
1909	The National Association for the Advancement of Colored People (NAACP) is founded.
1910–1934	Du Bois serves as director of publications and research at the NAACP. Du Bois founds and edits the *Crisis*, the monthly magazine of the NAACP.
1919	Du Bois calls for another Pan-African Congress for international racial equality, in Paris, France.
1934–1944	Du Bois becomes a sociology professor at Atlanta University.
1935	Du Bois's book *Black Reconstruction* is published.
1944–1948	Du Bois returns to the NAACP as director of special research.
1950	Nina Gomer Du Bois dies. Du Bois runs for the U.S. Senate as a candidate for the American Labor Party. Du Bois serves as director of the Peace Information Center. He is arrested, put on trial, and found innocent of criminal activities associated with the Peace Information Center.
1951	Shirley Graham and W.E.B. Du Bois are married.
1952	The U.S. government denies Du Bois a passport.
1958	Du Bois wins the Soviet Union's Lenin Prize for peace.
1958–1959	Du Bois travels around the world. As he tours he gives speeches and continues to write.
1961	Du Bois becomes a member of the Communist Party.
1963	Du Bois gives up his U.S. citizenship and becomes a citizen of Ghana. W.E.B. Du Bois dies on August 27 in Ghana at the age of ninety-five.

Glossary

abolition (a-buh-LIH-shun) The act of doing away with something such as slavery or segregation.

adhered (ad-HEERD) To have strictly followed or have observed the rules.

agitator (A-jih-tayt-er) A person who stirs up trouble or presses an issue in an attempt to get results.

allocation (a-luh-KAY-shun) Division for a specific purpose.

candidacy (CAN-did-eh-see) A person who is running for an elected position.

civil rights (SIH-vul RYTS) The freedoms and privileges one has as a citizen of a society, such as the right to vote and the right to free speech.

Civil War (SIH-vul WOR) A war between two sides within one country. In the United States, the Civil War was fought between the Northern and Southern states of America from 1861 to 1865.

commencement (kuh-MENS-ment) A ceremony or the day when degrees are given out to students who have completed their studies.

creed (KREED) A collection of beliefs.

diphtheria (dip-THEER-ee-uh) A serious illness of the throat, with symptoms that include high fever.

discrimination (dis-krih-mih-NAY-shun) Different treatment on a basis such as by skin color and not by individual merit or skill.

elite (ay-LEET) A small group of people in a larger group who have more power, privileges, or wealth than the rest of the group.

emancipation (ih-man-sih-PAY-shun) The act of freeing from restraint, control, or the power of another, usually referring to the freeing of slaves.

ghetto (GEH-toh) A section of a city where members of a minority group live together because of financial, social, or political limitations.

judicial (joo-DIH-shul) Relating to the function or administration of the court system.

livelihood (LYV-lee-hud) A method of supporting oneself to stay alive.

lynched (LYNCHT) Killed a person by mob action and without legal authority.

manifesto (ma-nih-FES-toh) A document that makes public the beliefs and intentions of a group of people.

masterful (MAS-ter-ful) To show evidence of possessing skill, power, or a strong will.

minstrel (MIN-strel) A performer that impersonates a black person, often using African American jokes and songs.

momentum (moh-MEN-tum) The gaining of energy or force through the progression of events.

oppression (uh-PREH-shun) The use of power over another.

persevering (per-seh-VEER-ing) Continuing with an action or undertaking despite opposition or discouragement.

Ph.D (P-H-D) An abbreviation for the Latin phrase *philosophiae doctor*, a degree given to someone who has completed advanced studies in a particular subject.

Plessy v. Ferguson (PLEH-see VER-sus FER-guh-sun) An 1896 U.S. Supreme Court case involving Homer Plessy, an African American who sat in a whites-only railroad car in Louisiana. Plessy was arrested. His defense in court was that a segregated railroad car violated his rights under the U.S. Constitution. Judge John Howard Ferguson ruled that the state of Louisiana had the authority to legalize segregated railroad cars within the state's borders. Plessy's appeal reached the Supreme Court, where the earlier decision was upheld.

prejudicial (PREH-joo-dish-ul) Showing dislike for a group of people different from you.

profoundly (pro-FOWND-lee) To have had an enormous affect on someone or something.

propaganda (prah-puh-GAN-duh) To increase the awareness of a person, an idea, or a cause, frequently by the use of written materials or a speech.

prophetic (prah-FEH-tik) To have predicted the future.

radical (RAD-i-kul) Having to do with an extreme change from the traditional or usual way of thinking or acting.

segregation (seh-gruh-GAY-shun) Enforced or voluntary separation or isolation by race, class, or culture.

separatism (SEH-pruh-tih-zum) A belief or idea of being apart from another.

singularly (SIN-gyuh-lur-lee) Exceptionally or extremely.

suffrage (SUH-frij) The right of voting.

suppression (seh-PREH-shun) The act of stopping a person or a group by force or authority.

surpassed (sur-PASD) To have gone beyond, in amount, quality, or degree.

terrorist (TER-er-ist) A person or group that seeks to scare or threaten with violence illegally.

tutelage (TOO-teh-lij) Education or instruction that is given to someone.

Victorian (vik-TOR-ee-an) Relating to or characteristic of the moral standards and attitudes of the age of Victoria, queen of England.

white supremacists (WYT suh-PREH-muh-sists) People who believe that white people are better than other racial or ethnic groups.

Additional Resources

If you would like to learn more about W.E.B. Du Bois, check out the following books and Web sites:

Books

McDaniel, Melissa. *W.E.B. Du Bois: Scholar and Civil Rights Activist*. New York: Grolier Publishing, 1999.

Turck, Mary. *The Civil Rights Movement for Kids: A History With 21 Activities*. Chicago, Illinois: Chicago Review Press, 2000.

Web Sites

Due to the changing nature of Internet links, PowerPlus Books has developed an online list of Web sites related to the subject of this book. This site is updated regularly. Please use this link to access the list: www.powerkidslinks.com/lalt/dubois/

Bibliography

Du Bois, William Edward Burghardt. *Autobiography of W.E.B. Du Bois: A Soliloquy on Viewing My Life from the Last Decade of Its First Century*. United States: International Publishers Co., Inc., 1997.

Du Bois, William Edward Burghardt. *The Souls of Black Folk*. New York: W. W. Norton & Company, 1999.

Horne, Gerald. *Black and Red: W.E.B. Du Bois and the Afro-American Response to the Cold War, 1944–1963*. Albany, NY: State University of New York Press, 1985.

Lewis, David Levering. *W.E.B. Du Bois: Biography of a Race, 1868–1919*. New York: Henry Holt and Company, 1993.

Lewis, David Levering. *W.E.B. Du Bois: The Fight for Equality and the American Century 1919–1963*. New York: Henry Holt and Company, 2000.

Lewis, David Levering. *W.E.B. Du Bois: A Reader*. New York: Henry Holt and Company, 1995.

McDaniel, Melissa. *W.E.B. Du Bois: Scholar and Civil Rights Activist*. New York: Grolier Publishing, 1999.

Stafford, Mark. *W.E.B. Du Bois: Scholar and Activist*. New York: Chelsea House, 1989.

Wexler, Sanford. *An Eyewitness History of the Civil Rights Movement*. New York: Checkmark Books, 1999.

Index

About the Author

Ryan P. Randolph is a freelance writer with an avid interest in history. Ryan has a bachelor of arts degree in both history and political science from Colgate University in Hamilton, New York. He has written several history books for children. He currently works in a strategic consulting and research firm that specializes in the financial services industry and lives with his wife in Mount Vernon, New York.

About the Consultant

Gerald Horne is the Moores Professor of History & African American Studies at the University of Houston in Texas. He is the author of several books, including *Race Woman: The Lives of Shirley Graham Du Bois* (New York University Press, 2000).

Primary Sources

Cover. W.E.B. Du Bois, photograph, 1918, C.M. Battey, Library of Congress Prints and Photographs Division; Background. *Crisis*, Vol. 1, Number 2 cover from December 1910, Special Collections and Archives, W.E.B. Du Bois Library, University of Massachusetts Amherst. **Page 4**. Du Bois at the Paris Exposition, photograph, 1900, Special Collections and Archives, W.E.B. Du Bois Library, University of Massachusetts Amherst. **Page 7**. Silent protest parade in New York [City] against the East St. Louis riots, photograph, 1917, Library of Congress Prints and Photographs Division. **Page 10**. *Great Barrington, Massachusetts*, lithograph, circa 1884, Published and drawn by L. R. Burleigh. Beck and Pauli, lithograph, Library of Congress Geography and Map Division. **Page 11**. Mary Silvina Burghardt Du Bois with her son W.E.B. Du Bois, photograph, circa 1868, Special Collections and Archives, W.E.B. Du Bois Library, University of Massachusetts Amherst. **Page 12**. *Arrival of the Dutch Leaders in Guinea: The Negotiation for the Purchase of Slaves Destined to be Sold Back to the Spanish Conquistadors*, engraving, circa 1585, Theodore de Bry, Bibliotheque Nationale, Paris. **Page 14**. Alfred Du Bois, photograph, Special Collections and Archives, W.E.B. Du Bois Library, University of Massachusetts Amherst. **Page 17**. Great Barrington High School Class of 1884, photograph, 1884, Special Collections and Archives, W.E.B. Du Bois Library, University of Massachusetts Amherst. **Page 19**. "Great Barrington Briefs" from Sept. 23, 1883, published in the September 29, 1883 edition of the New York *Globe*, W.E.B. Du Bois. **Page 22**. Faculty and students outside Jubilee Hall, Fisk University, photograph, circa 1887, image altered to add inset of Du Bois, Special Collections and Archives, W.E.B. Du Bois Library, University of Massachusetts Amherst. **Page 24**. Wilson County, Tennessee teaching contract made out to Du Bois on June 11, 1887, Special Collections and Archives, W.E.B. Du Bois Library, University of Massachusetts Amherst. **Page 26**. *The shackle broken – by the genius of freedom*, lithograph, 1874, Edward Sachse & Co., Library of Congress Prints and Photographs Division. **Page 27**. William James, photograph, Harvard University. **Page 28**. Harvard Graduation portrait, photograph, circa 1890, Special Collections and Archives, W.E.B. Du Bois Library, University of Massachusetts Amherst. **Page 29**. University of Berlin, Germany, photograph, circa 1900, Library of Congress Prints and Photographs Division. **Page 30**. "Mitglieds-Karte" Admission card signed by the economist Gustav Schmoller admitting Du Bois to his seminar at the University of Berlin, Winter, 1893-94, Special Collections and Archives, W.E.B. Du Bois Library, University of Massachusetts Amherst. **Page 32**. Gore Hall, Harvard, photograph, 1901. **Page 34**. Nina Gomer Du Bois, photograph, 1910, Special Collections and Archives, W.E.B. Du Bois Library, University of Massachusetts Amherst. **Page 35**. *Northwestern corner of Eleventh and Pine Streets*, watercolor, 1883, Benjamin R. Evans, The Library Company Philadelphia. **Page 36**. Burghardt Du Bois at eight months, photograph, circa 1898, image has been cropped, Special Collections and Archives, W.E.B. Du Bois Library, University of Massachusetts Amherst. **Page 39**. Letter from Nina Du Bois to W.E.B. Du Bois dated January 5, 1902, Special Collections and Archives, W.E.B. Du Bois Library, University of Massachusetts Amherst. **Page 41**. "Arthur Jordan . . . hung by men unknown at Warrenton . . . 2 o'clock a.m. Monday Jan. 19th 1880," pencil-on-paper diary entry, Dr. Gustavus Richard Brown Horner, Papers of G.W.B. Horner (#379), Special Collections, University of Virginia Library. **Page 43**. *The Souls of Black Folk: Essays and Sketches*, first-edition frontispiece and title page, 1903, W.E.B. Du Bois, Chicago: A. C. McClurg & Co, courtesy of Northwestern University. **Page 45**. The map of Africa by treaty, 1909, Sir E.

Hertslet, printed for H. M. Stationery Off. by Harrison and sons, London, color-key to map enlarged by Rosen Publishing Group, Library of Congress Geography and Map Division. **Page 46**. Speakers at the 1921 Second Pan African Congress, photograph, Special Collections and Archives, W.E.B. Du Bois Library, University of Massachusetts Amherst. **Page 49**. Booker T. Washington, 1903, photograph, Cheynes Studio, Hampton, Virginia, Library of Congress Prints and Photographs Division. **Page 50**. Ida Wells-Barnett, newspaper illustration, 1891, I. Garland Penn, Library of Congress Rare Book and Special Collections Division. **Page 53**. Niagara Conference, photograph, 1905, image was altered to add inset of Du Bois, Special Collections and Archives, W.E.B. Du Bois Library, University of Massachusetts Amherst. **Page 54**. Depiction of the 1906 Atlanta race riot published in the October 7, 1906 *Le Petit Journal*, courtesy of the Atlanta History Center. **Page 55**. "From the Point of View of the Negro," editorial from the November 1906 *World Today*, Du Bois. **Page 58–59**. Du Bois and members of the *Crisis* staff in their New York office, photograph, circa 1911, Courtesy of the NYPL Schomburg Center. **Page 60**. (*See cover, background*) **Page 62**. *True Sons of Freedom*, chromolithograph poster, 1918, Gustrine Chas, Library of Congress Prints and Photographs Division. **Page 65**. *The Signing of Peace in the Hall of Mirrors, Versailles, 28th June 1919*, oil painting, circa 1920, Sir William Orpen, Imperial War Museum. **Page 66**. Marcus Garvey, photograph, 1923, Toussaint Studios, Library of Congress Prints and Photographs Division. **Page 68**. *Street Life, Harlem*, circa 1940, oil painting, William H. Johnson, Smithsonian American Art Museum, Washington, D.C. **Page 69**. Bridal Party of Nina Yolande Du Bois, photograph, 1928, Special Collections and Archives, W.E.B. Du Bois Library, University of Massachusetts Amherst. **Page 71**. *The Unemployed, Charleston*, etching, circa 1930, Elizabeth O'Neill Verner, Library of Congress Prints and Photographs Division. **Page 74**. Walter White, photograph, circa 1930, Library of Congress Prints and Photographs Division. **Page 76**. *The Freedmen's Union Industrial School*, Richmond, Va., engraving, 1866, James E. Taylor, from *Frank Leslie's Illustrated Newspaper*, v. 23, 1866 Sept. 22, p. 5, Library of Congress Prints and Photographs Division. **Page 81**. Lenin Peace Prize awarded to Du Bois in 1958, Special Collections and Archives, W.E.B. Du Bois Library, University of Massachusetts Amherst. **Page 84**. Session of the House Un-American Activities Committee held on October 21, 1947, Library of Congress Prints and Photographs Division. **Page 85**. Shirley Graham Du Bois and W.E.B. Du Bois, photograph, February 23, 1955, Special Collections and Archives, W.E.B. Du Bois Library, University of Massachusetts Amherst. **Page 86**. American Labor Party Candidate Dr. W.E.B. Du Bois running for the U.S. Senate, campaign flyer, 1950, Special Collections and Archives, W.E.B. Du Bois Library, University of Massachusetts Amherst. **Page 87**. Vito Marcantonio, photograph, 1941, Library of Congress Prints and Photographs Division. **Page 88**. World Peace Appeal petition issued by the World Committee in Defence of Peace in Stockholm in March 1950, Special Collections and Archives, W.E.B. Du Bois Library, University of Massachusetts Amherst. **Page 91**. W.E.B. Du Bois's passport, stamped with entry dates from 1960 and 1961, Special Collections and Archives, W.E.B. Du Bois Library, University of Massachusetts Amherst. **Page 92**. Du Bois and Chairman Mao Tse-tung, photograph, 1959, Special Collections and Archives, W.E.B. Du Bois Library, University of Massachusetts Amherst. **Page 93**. Rosa Parks being fingerprinted by Deputy Sheriff D. H. Lackey in Montgomery, Alabama, photograph, 1956, Library of Congress Prints and Photographs Division. **Page 95**. President Kwame Nkrumah toasts Du Bois on his ninety-fifth birthday, photograph, February 1963, Special Collections and Archives, W.E.B. Du Bois Library, University of Massachusetts Amherst. **Page 97**. March on Washington, photograph, August 28, 1963, Library of Congress Prints and Photographs Division. **Page 98**. W.E.B. Du Bois's state funeral, photograph, August 1963, Special Collections and Archives, W.E.B. Du Bois Library, University of Massachusetts Amherst.

Credits

Photo Credits

Cover, pp. 7, 26, 29, 49, 62, 66, 71, 74, 76, 84, 87, 93, 97 Library of Congress Prints and Photographs Division; cover background, pp. 4, 11, 14, 17, 22, 24, 28, 30, 34, 36, 39, 46, 53, 60, 69, 81, 85, 86, 88, 91, 92, 95, 98 Special Collections and Archives, W.E.B. Du Bois Library, University of Massachusetts Amherst; pp. 10, 45 Library of Congress Geography and Map Division; p.12 Bibliotheque Nationale, Paris/Giraudon/Bridgeman Art Library; p. 27 © Bettmann/CORBIS; p. 35 The Library Company Philadelphia; p. 41 Papers of G.W.B. Horner (#379), Special Collections, University of Virginia Library; p. 43 courtesy of Northwestern University; p. 50 Library of Congress, Rare Book and Special Collections Division; p. 54 Courtesy of the Atlanta History Center; pp. 58–59 Courtesy of the NYPL Schomburg Center; p. 65 The Art Archive/Imperial War Museum; p. 68 © Smithsonian American Art Museum, Washington, DC/Art Resource, NY.

Project Editor
Daryl Heller

Series Design
Laura Murawski

Layout Design
Corinne L. Jacob
Maria Melendez
Ginny Chu

Photo Researcher
Jeffrey Wendt